Bernd T. Meyer

Speech recognition by man and machine

Bernd T. Meyer

Speech recognition by man and machine

Influence of speaking rate, style, and effort on the recognition performance of human listeners and automatic classifiers

Südwestdeutscher Verlag für Hochschulschriften

Impressum/Imprint (nur für Deutschland/ only for Germany)

Bibliografische Information der Deutschen Nationalbibliothek: Die Deutsche Nationalbibliothek verzeichnet diese Publikation in der Deutschen Nationalbibliografie; detaillierte bibliografische Daten sind im Internet über http://dnb.d-nb.de abrufbar.

Alle in diesem Buch genannten Marken und Produktnamen unterliegen warenzeichen-, marken- oder patentrechtlichem Schutz bzw. sind Warenzeichen oder eingetragene Warenzeichen der jeweiligen Inhaber. Die Wiedergabe von Marken, Produktnamen, Gebrauchsnamen, Handelsnamen, Warenbezeichnungen u.s.w. in diesem Werk berechtigt auch ohne besondere Kennzeichnung nicht zu der Annahme, dass solche Namen im Sinne der Warenzeichen- und Markenschutzgesetzgebung als frei zu betrachten wären und daher von jedermann benutzt werden dürften.

Verlag: Südwestdeutscher Verlag für Hochschulschriften GmbH & Co. KG
Dudweiler Landstr. 99, 66123 Saarbrücken, Deutschland
Telefon +49 681 37 20 271-1, Telefax +49 681 37 20 271-0
Email: info@svh-verlag.de
Zugl.: Oldenburg, Carl-von-Ossietzky Universität, Diss., 2010

Herstellung in Deutschland:
Schaltungsdienst Lange o.H.G., Berlin
Books on Demand GmbH, Norderstedt
Reha GmbH, Saarbrücken
Amazon Distribution GmbH, Leipzig
ISBN: 978-3-8381-2155-0

Imprint (only for USA, GB)

Bibliographic information published by the Deutsche Nationalbibliothek: The Deutsche Nationalbibliothek lists this publication in the Deutsche Nationalbibliografie; detailed bibliographic data are available in the Internet at http://dnb.d-nb.de.

Any brand names and product names mentioned in this book are subject to trademark, brand or patent protection and are trademarks or registered trademarks of their respective holders. The use of brand names, product names, common names, trade names, product descriptions etc. even without a particular marking in this works is in no way to be construed to mean that such names may be regarded as unrestricted in respect of trademark and brand protection legislation and could thus be used by anyone.

Publisher: Südwestdeutscher Verlag für Hochschulschriften GmbH & Co. KG
Dudweiler Landstr. 99, 66123 Saarbrücken, Germany
Phone +49 681 37 20 271-1, Fax +49 681 37 20 271-0
Email: info@svh-verlag.de

Printed in the U.S.A.
Printed in the U.K. by (see last page)
ISBN: 978-3-8381-2155-0

Abstract

Despite several decades of research, automatic speech recognition (ASR) lacks the performance achieved by human listeners. One of the major challenges in ASR is to cope with the immense variability of spoken language, which can be categorized into extrinsic sources (e.g., additive noise) and intrinsic factors (such as speaking rate, style, effort, dialect, and accent). What can we learn from the biological blueprint, and which cues important in human speech recognition (HSR) should be considered to improve ASR performance? The scope of this thesis is to answer these questions by comparing the HSR and ASR performance and - based on these results - to suggest an alternative way of feature extraction to improve ASR. The comparison is based on the Oldenburg Logatome Corpus, which is a database that contains simple nonsense words consisting of phoneme triplets and which covers the intrinsic variations mentioned above.

The man-machine-gap in terms of the signal-to-noise ratio (SNR) was estimated to be 15 dB, i.e., the masking level in ASR has to be lowered by 15 dB to achieve the same performance as human listeners. The contributions to this gap could be attributed to the individual processing steps of the ASR system: The information loss caused by the feature extraction resulted in an SNR-equivalent information loss of 10 dB, while suboptimal classification accounted for the remaining 5 dB of the overall gap. Moreover, the analysis of intrinsic variations showed that human listeners are superior to ASR systems in exploiting temporal cues. These findings motivated the use of spectro-temporal Gabor features in ASR, which were found to exhibit increased robustness against a wide range of noise types. In the presence of *intrinsic* variations of speech, Gabor features increase the overall performance regarding several factors (such as speaking effort and style), which suggests to incorporate both spectro-temporal and temporal cues in future ASR systems.

Contents

Contents

1

General introduction

Spoken language is the most important form of human communication. Despite several decades of research, the recognition of speech by machines lacks the superior performance achieved by humans (Lippmann, 1997; Sroka and Braida, 2005; Meyer et al., 2007; Cooke and Scharenborg, 2008). One of the reasons for the outstanding performance of human listeners is the robustness against the variability in speech, i.e., the invariance of the recognition of speech containing such variations. The variability can be categorized in extrinsic factors (such as additive or channel noise) and intrinsic factors, which are associated with speech itself and do not arise from external factors. Among these factors are the speaker's gender, age, physiology, the speaking rate and style, dialect, accent, co-articulation, and vocal effort. Most of these factors were found to severely degrade the performance of automatic speech recognition (ASR), i.e., the conversion of spoken utterances into text (Benzeguiba et al., 2007). For example, changes in speaking rate increase the error rates of ASR, which indicates that intrinsic factors have to be considered in auditory modeling in order to close the gap that is observed between human speech recognition (HSR) and ASR (Siegler and Stern, 1995). This thesis is motivated by these observations, and covers two main aspects: 1.) How does the presence of intrinsic variations (speaking rate, style, effort, dialect and accent) compared to normally spoken utterances influence HSR and ASR, and what are the specific differences between these two? 2.) Can biologically-inspired features which account for cues that are employed by human listeners and which are based on the comparison of HSR and ASR help to decrease the man-machine-gap in speech recognition?

1.1 Difficulties in automatic speech recognition

The advances in ASR during the last decade have allowed for the use of this technology in several fields, including dictation systems, dialogue systems in telecommunication for small or medium vocabularies, and support for people with disabilities. Despite this progress, ASR technology is not widely used in our everyday life, although it offers numerous advantages compared to traditional keyboard input, such as a high data rate that can be achieved even by untrained speakers and its use in hands-free applications. Another example is the use of ASR in hand-held devices that might be used to support hearing-impaired listeners in one-to-many communications (Woodcock, 1997).

The recognition of speech is a task that is easily performed by human listeners in everyday situations. In this context, it may seem surprising that technological advances have not yet resulted in a system that automatically performs this task with the same reliability. However, the production and recognition of speech are highly complex processes that involve high-order active processing using implicit knowledge of spoken language. The difficulties encountered in today's speech recognition systems may therefore appear more comprehensible, especially when considering that "spoken language is the most sophisticated behavior of the most complex organism in the known universe" (Roger K. Moore). Due to the co-evolution of speech production and reception organs, it can be assumed that both production and perception are very well tuned processes, thus resulting in internal representations in the auditory system that optimally characterize the speech sound and its underlying message.

The issues that need to be considered in ASR can be roughly divided into four categories (Schukat-Talamazzini, 1995), as illustrated in Fig. 1.1: The continuity of speech arises from the fact that speech in general lacks visible boundaries or markers which would allow for an easy segmentation of the speech units that need to be identified. The complexity of a speech recognition task depends, among other factors, on the speaking style (e.g., conversational vs. formal speech), which influences the number of pattern alternatives that have to be considered for classification. Other parameters that contribute to the complexity are the size of vocabulary and the number of speakers (speaker-specific recognition vs. speaker-independent ASR), which result in increased computational costs (due to the larger number of comparisons of spoken and stored speech patterns) and require larger amounts of training data and storage capacity for the auditory models. The mapping of sub-word sequences to words or sentences is not a trivial problem due to the ambiguity of language, even when sub-word units such as phonemes are perfectly classified. For example, the ambiguity between the questions "How to wreck a nice beach?" and "How to recognize speech?" that consist of very similar sequences of phonemes needs to be resolved based on high-level knowledge. In human hearing, this knowledge is not limited to efficient language models, but also includes information about the a-priori probabilities of properties of the signal to be recognized and sources of noise in a specific acoustical scene (i.e., the "world-knowledge"). Finally, the immense variability that is present in spoken language aggravates the correct classification of speech. This variability results in the fact that not even the same speaker can reproduce an utterance exactly, and ranges from speaker-specific, intrinsic factors (e.g., physiological parameters, dialect, age, health condition,) over intrinsic parameters that are subject to continuous changes (speaking rate, speaking effort, emotion) to extrinsic sources of variability, such as competing talkers or reverberation.

1.2 Comparing speech recognition of men and machines

The observation of the excellent performance of the human listeners compared to automatic recognizers has inspired many works that aim at the goal of improving ASR by copying the relevant signal processing capabilities of the auditory system. A classic study that reviewed HSR and ASR performance on comparable tasks was presented by Lippmann (1997). Lippmann reported that error rates in ASR - when performing complex tasks, such as the recognition of conversational speech - were an order of magnitude higher than those of human listeners. Research that relates to these observations was conducted to improve the feature extraction stage in ASR systems, often by relying on observations from physiological findings of the auditory system and/or by using the output of auditory HSR models (Kleinschmidt, 2002; Kleinschmidt and Gelbart, 2002; Cooke, 2005; Chiu and Stern, 2008; Domont et al., 2008; Chiu et al., 2009). Recently, the topic of man-machine-comparison was covered in research analyzing a large variety of tasks such as the recognition of phonemes in non-stationary noise (Cooke and Scharenborg, 2008), in high- and lowpass-filtered signals (Sroka and Braida, 2005), the differences in language modeling (Shen et al., 2008), as well as studies that take the complete speech processing chain into account by application of

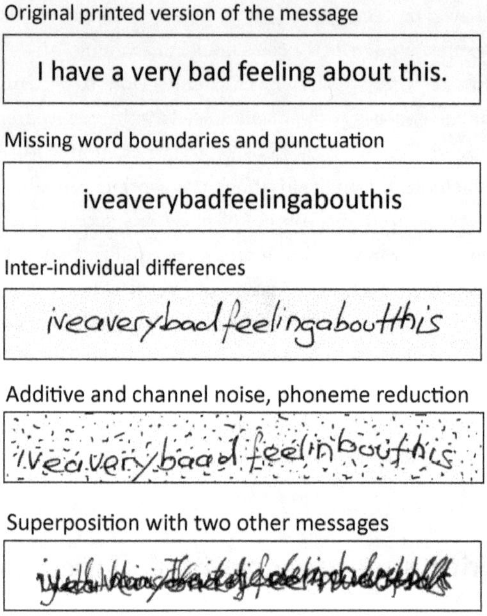

Original printed version of the message

> ## I have a very bad feeling about this.

Missing word boundaries and punctuation

> ### iveaverybadfeelingabouthis

Inter-individual differences

> *iveaverybadfeelingaboutthis*

Additive and channel noise, phoneme reduction

> *iveaverybaad feelinbouthis*

Superposition with two other messages

FIG. 1.1 *Illustration the problems that arise in ASR (by comparing ASR and the problem of optical character recognition), adapted from (Schukat-Talamazzini, 1995). While the original (printed) version of the sentence is easily readable, the hand-written last sentence with simulated two-talker babble can hardly be deciphered.*

ASR-techniques to build an end-to-end model of human word recognition (Scharenborg, 2005).

In (Scharenborg, 2007), the research fields of HSR and ASR were compared, and closer interaction between these was promoted. A stronger collaboration between these research areas does not only hold potential for the improvement of ASR: A second beneficial effect of man-machine-comparison is that it may be employed in modeling human speech perception (see Fig. 1.2). While the features of conventional recognition systems are based on the spectral envelope of short-time spectral representations that account for properties of hearing only to a limited extent (Hunt, 1999), it can be assumed that error patterns of men and machines are more consistent when similar signal extraction techniques are applied (e.g., by extraction of ASR features based on auditory models). While this thesis is concerned with an improvement of ASR based on knowledge derived from HSR, the results from a man-machine-comparison may serve as basis for the development of new approaches in the design of perception models based on ASR technology.

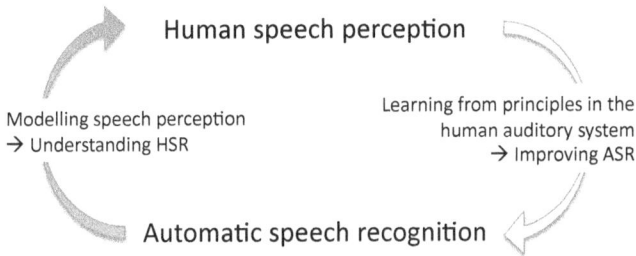

Human speech perception

Modelling speech perception
→ Understanding HSR

Learning from principles in the human auditory system
→ Improving ASR

Automatic speech recognition

FIG. 1.2 *A stronger interchange between the research fields of HSR and ASR could on the one hand result in improvements of ASR (by transferring principles from the human auditory system to automatic recognizers). On the other hand, HSR may profit from ASR research, since the use of features inspired by the human auditory system is likely to result in more human-like errors. This aspect may therefore contribute to improved models of human speech perception and an evaluation of these.*

1.3 Top-down vs. bottom-up processing

The robustness of human speech perception and consequently the excellent performance in speech recognition presumably arises from two basic steps involved in the construction of auditory objects (Bregman, 1994): First, a neuronal internal representation is generated based on stimulus-driven processing that involves no higher-order cortical processing ("bottom-up processing"). Secondly, a hypothesis-driven process relying on the world-knowledge and factors such as selective attentiveness retroact on the internal representations ("top-down processing"). This scheme can be compared to the technical approaches applied in ASR, where features are extracted from speech signals ("bottom-up") and are subsequently compared to stored (or learned) representations during the classification process ("top-down"). The human-machine-gap may therefore be divided into a top-down and a bottom-up component by presenting to human listeners utterances, which are informationally equivalent to ASR features. When the complete ASR feature information is made accessible to listeners, the resulting degradation (compared to the original signals) quantifies the gap caused by imperfect speech features. On the other hand, the differences between HSR with resynthesized features and ASR are a measure for the gap in top-down-processing (due to imperfect world-knowledge-based classification). One of the questions covered in this thesis is what the contributions of low-level feature extraction and high-level classification are to the overall differences between human and automatic speech recognition.

1.4 Structure of this work

This work is structured as follows: Chapter 2 analyzes the effect of speech-intrinsic variations on human speech recognition. The measurements with human listeners were performed with the Oldenburg Logatome Corpus, which is a speech database containing short non-sense utterances that were recorded with several systematically varied intrinsic variations, i.e., different speaking rates, speaking effort (loudly vs. softly spoken speech) and speaking style (utterances spoken normally and as a question). Furthermore, the influence of speaker-specific variabilities is covered by using dialectal and accented speech as speech stimuli. The design considerations and recording conditions, as well as a detailed description of the audio material contained in the database is presented. Additionally, a simple model based on the spectral distance between long-term phoneme spectra and the masking noise is proposed to explain for the observed differences in recognition and error rates in human speech recognition.

The results obtained in tests with human listeners comprise the basis for the man-machine-comparison, which is introduced in Chapter 3. The experiments are designed to enable a fair comparison by using the logatome database both for HSR and ASR. Standard ASR features are resynthesized to audible speech tokens, which are presented to human listeners. By using stimuli that contain the same information that is accessible to ASR, the human-machine-gap is separated into a top-down and a bottom-up component, as discussed above. The effect of intrinsic variations is analyzed for both HSR conditions and for ASR.

Chapter 4 presents ASR experiments based on a front-end that extracts spectro-temporal information from the speech signal (Kleinschmidt, 2002), which is motivated by the results of the man-machine-comparison and physiological findings from the primary auditory cortex. The feature extraction is performed with optimized Gabor filters (Meyer and Kollmeier, 2008) and compared to cepstral coefficients. Similarly to the experiments in Chapters 2 and 3, the Oldenburg Logatome database is used for the tests, which enables a detailed analysis of the effect of speech-intrinsic variations.

2

Human phoneme recognition as a function of speech-intrinsic variabilities

Abstract

The influence of speech-intrinisic variations (speaking rate, effort, style and dialect or accent) on human speech perception was investigated. In listening experiments with 16 listeners, confusions of consonant-vowel-consonant (CVC) and vowel-consonant-vowel (VCV) sounds in speech-weighted noise were analyzed. Experiments were based on the OLLO logatome speech database, which was designed for a man-machine comparison. It contains utterances spoken by 50 speakers from five dialect/accent regions and covers several intrinsic variations. By comparing results depending on intrinsic and extrinsic variations (i.e., different levels of masking noise), the degradation induced by variabilities can be expressed in terms of the SNR. The spectral level distance between the respective speech segment and the long-term spectrum of the masking noise was found to be a good predictor for recognition rates, while phoneme confusions were influenced by the distance to spectrally close phonemes. An analysis based on transmitted information of articulatory features showed that voicing and manner of articulation are comparatively robust cues in the presence of intrinsic variations, whereas the coding of place is more degraded. The database and detailed results have been made available for comparisons between human speech recognition (HSR) and automatic speech recognizers (ASR).

2.1 Introduction

Normal human listeners exhibit an excellent performance in speech recognition despite the immense variations present in spoken language. This holds even if different speakers have to be understood, i.e., human listeners can compensate for a variety of speaking rates, different regional accents and different vocal effort of the received speech.

The robustness to these underlying speech intrinsic variabilities is a major achievement of human speech recognition (HSR) that is not well understood yet. Many sources of variation in spoken language have been observed and well documented in several studies, such as, for example the gender and age of the talker (male versus female speaker versus children speech (Hazan and Markham, 2004)), the effect of certain speaking styles (such as, e. g., speaking clearly to achieve a higher intelligibility (Krause and Braida, 2003)), and the influence of dialect and accent on speech intelligibility (Li, 2003). Other factors that may influence speaking rate and effort are, e.g., emotion, stress, fatigue, and health condition. These sources of variation are not independent, an example being the influence of speaking rate on pronunciation that arises from deletions, insertions, and coarticulation (Fosler-Lussier and Morgan, 1999). Despite the large number of studies dealing with variations in speech, it is still unclear how the auditory system manages to produce percepts that are largely invariant to such changes in speech.

While the robustness of automatic speech recognition (ASR) against extrinsic variabilities (such as channel transmission properties and additive or convolutive noise) has been studied in detail in the past (Hermansky and Morgan, 1997; Stern et al., 1996; Tchorz and Kollmeier, 1999; Cooke et al., 2001), it is far less understood in which way ASR also suffers from a lack of robustness towards "intrinsic" variations of speech (that is, speaker, gender, speech rate, vocal effort, regional accents, speaking style and non stationarity). Various methods that increase the robustness of ASR towards some variations of speech have successfully been used for several years (an example being techniques that compensate for the shift of formant frequencies caused by variations of vocal-tract length). Recently, however, much of the research is devoted to broader classes of variabilities, with the aim of understanding the influence of speech-intrinsic variations on automatic speech recognition, and to build feature extraction or classfication methods invariant to these variations (Mori et al., 2007). Similarly, several researchers focused on the comparison of the recognition performance of human listeners and ASR (Lippmann, 1997; Sroka and Braida, 2005; Ten Bosch and Kirchhoff, 2007; Cooke and Scharenborg, 2008). On a phoneme recognition task, Meyer et al. (2007) found similar overall results for HSR and ASR when the signal-to-noise ratio was 15 dB higher for the automatic recognizer. This value depends on the type of experiment to be compared across men and machines. Such comparisons highlight the deficiencies of current automatic recognizers in the presence of extrinsic and intrinsic variations of spoken language.

Since understanding the principles of human speech recognition (HSR) may help to improve performance of ASR (Allen, 1994), it is therefore desirable to study the influence of speech variabilities on human speech recognition as a baseline for making ASR more robust against these variabilities. For example, it was shown that error rates increase when speaking rates deviate from normal (i.e., average) speaking rate. Siegler and Stern (1995) reported an increase of ASR error rates by a factor of three, when the rate of speech deviated more than two standard deviations from the average rate. The effect of conversational speech was investigated by Weintraub et al. (1996) who found that error rates doubled when conversational speech is compared to a read, clearly uttered version of the same speech material.

However, it is often difficult to compare findings from different HSR and ASR studies due to the existing variability across speech and speakers in the available speech databases and the lack of appropriate speech corpora that are suitable both for human speech recognition and ASR experiments while providing the possibility to study the effect of intrinsic variations of speech: Some of the available speech databases are suitable for both human speech recognition and ASR experiments, while others provide the possibility to study the effect of intrinsic variations of speech either on HSR or on ASR.

In this study, we therefore perform HSR experiments to assess the impact of several intrinsic variabilities of spoken language that are contained in the same speech database suitable both for HSR and ASR experiments. This database consists of a CVC and VCV logatome corpus (the so-called "Oldenburg Logatome Corpus" (OLLO), where 'logatome' refers to a word that has no semantic meaning, but is correctly composed with respect to phonetic and phonotactic rules). By using simple nonsense phoneme combinations, the focus is laid on a basic recognition task that does not rely on high-level lexical knowledge. Such recognition can primarily be considered as a bottom-up sensory one-out-of-N discrimination task in HSR that requires no prior knowledge of the language structure and a low cognitive load imposed on the subjects when performing the task. In ASR the recognition task requires templates or word models primarily on the acoustical feature layer without a suprasegmental or language model to be fitted to the speech data. Hence, the OLLO database can be used as a reference for HSR research as well as for comparing ASR experiments using the same speech elements. Moreover, the influence of speech variabilities on both types of experiments can easily be studied. The principles underlying the database construction and its recording will be discussed.

The primary aim of the current paper is to establish the baseline for HSR experiments with the OLLO corpus that can be utilized in future work for comparison with ASR. To do so, the influence of speaking style (i. e., fast, slow, soft, loud) as well as of speaker-specific factors (gender and dialect region) on human speech recognition is studied with a total number of 16 listeners and 120 hrs of listening experiments. Speakers originating from various dialect regions in Germany, as well as from the French-spaking part of Belgium, have been recorded to study the effect of dialect and accent. Since all phonemes in the database occur both in German and English language, the utterances may also be of useful for listening tests with English subjects. The results presented in this study were obtained with German listeners. Even though some differences in average recognition rates from the mentioned variabilities are expected (especially when the experiment is performed in noise which is necessary to avoid any ceiling effect), it is unclear if these differences are due to the deterioration of specific speech features or due to a general, unsystematic decrease in intelligibility. For this reason, a speech transmission analysis (Miller and Nicely, 1955; Wang and Bilger, 1973) should be performed that studies the transmission of acoustic speech features (such as, e. g. average spectrum of the phonemes to be recognized or articulatory features) as a function of underlying speech variabilities. In order to cancel out the individual influence of each individual listener, such an analysis only makes sense if an appropriate amount of data is available that can be averaged across subjects. Hence, the number of subjects was selected to be sufficiently high to derive valid conclusions for these aspects of HSR.

This paper is structured as follows: In Section 2.2, a detailed description of the Oldenburg Logatome speech database is presented. The measurement setup, parameters for the listening tests and outcome measures for data analysis are described in Section 2.3. Overall results and effects of variabilities on information transmission are presented in Section 2.4. Sections 2.5 and 2.6 contain the discussion of results, a summary and the conclusions.

2.2 Description of the database

2.2.1 Choice of phonemes and speech stimuli

The corpus used for this study should contain speech with labeled, speech-intrinsic variabilities. The experiments aim at the simple task of phoneme recognition without the possibility to exploit context knowledge. An analyis of coarticulation effects and easy determination of phoneme recognition rates are further desirable properties. Short combinations of phonemes satisfy all of these pre-requisites. We chose combinations of vowel-consonant-vowel (VCV) and consonant-vowel-consonant (CVC) with identical outer phonemes for the database. The standard recognition task for those non-sense utterances or logatomes is to identify the middle phoneme, which limits the number of response alternatives and allows for an easy realization of HSR tests. Since the OLLO corpus should be suitable for a comparison of speech recognition by human listeners and automatic speech recognizers, the choice of phonemes was based on HSR and ASR recognition experiments. Phonemes that are critical in either human or automatic recognition of speech were selected, so that significant differences in recognition rates may already be obtained with smaller test sets.

Critical phonemes in human speech recognition

The results of monosyllabic and bisyllabic rhyme tests with normal-hearing listeners were analyzed to determine the phonemes which are most often confused by human listeners in English or German (Dubno and Levitt, 1981; Gelfand et al., 1985; Mueller, 1992; Kliem, 1993). The results suggest that ten consonant phonemes /b/, /d/, /f/, /g/, /k/, /l/, /p/, /r/, /s/, /v/) and seven vowel phonemes (/ae/, /ɛ/, /i/, /ɪ/, /u/, /ʊ/, /u/, /y/) should be taken into account.

Critical phonemes in ASR

In order to determine the critical phonemes in ASR, phoneme confusions from a recognition experiment were analyzed: Spectro-temporal ASR features (Kleinschmidt and

Gelbart, 2002) served as input to a non-linear neural network (multi-layer perceptron, MLP) that was trained and tested using a phoneme-labeled speech database (TIMIT). Results were analyzed on a frame-by-frame basis and phonemes were sorted by their relative error rate. Eight phonemes ($/d/$, $/v/$, $/f/$, $/g/$, $/z/$, $/m/$, $/n/$, $/ʃ/$) were selected for the corpus because they appear in both German and English language, produced high error rates in the experiment and are often present in phoneme confusions.

Final set of phonemes

The final number of phonemes to be considered was limited by the required time to record all necessary items with a single speaker. Since the standard recognition task for the OLLO database is to identify the middle phoneme, not all possible combinations of consonant and vowel phonemes were taken into account. The final phoneme set for VCVs consists of five vowel phonemes and 14 consonant phonemes (cf. Table 2.1. The set for CVCs contains one of ten vowels and one of eight consonants. A combination of these phonemes results in a total of 150 different logatomes (70 VCVs, 80 CVCs). The vowels are genuinely different with respect to height, backness and roundedness (i.e. their constituent features in the cardinal vowel system (MacArthur, 1992)), with the exception of $/a/$ and $/a:/$, which differ only by a suprasegmental indicating different phoneme durations.

2.2.2 Variabilities and speakers

The choice of variabilities was based on ASR experiments with annotated test corpora that compared the performance of automatic recognizers with these variabilities present or not. The variabilities under consideration included speaker's gender, age and dialect, speaking style/effort (which also relates to pitch), rate of speech, and breathing noise. The largest impact on performance was observed for the variabilities speaking rate (fast vs. slow), speaking style (affirmation vs. question), speaking effort (loud vs. soft), and dialect/accent. The latter was integrated in the database by including logatomes of dialect speakers from different regions of Germany and from the French-speaking part of Belgium. Ten speakers originating from the northern part of Germany (Oldenburg near Bremen and Hanover) were recorded. The spoken language in this region is usually considered as standard German (Kohler, 1995). We will refer to this category as 'no dialect' (ND). Subjects with dialect originated from the Northern part of Germany

Number of speakers	50 (25 male, 25 female)
Number of different VCVs	70 (five outer vowels (/a/, /ɛ/, /ɪ/, /ɔ/, /ʊ/) combined with 14 central consonants (/b/, /d/, /f/, /g/, /k/, /l/, /m/, /n/, /p/, /s/, /ʃ/, /t/, /v/, /ts/))
Number of different CVCs	80 (eight outer consonants (/b/, /d/, /f/, /g/, /k/, /p/, /s/, /t/) combined with 10 central vowels (/a/, /ɛ/, /ɪ/, /ɔ/, /ʊ/, /aː/, /e/, /i/, /o/, /u/))
Number of different logatomes	150
Number of speaking styles	5 + reference condition 'normal' (fast, slow, loud, soft, question)
Number of dialects/accents	4 + reference condition 'no dialect' (East Frisian, Bavarian, East Phalian, French)
Utterances per speaker	2,700 (150 logatomes x 3 repetitions x 6 speaking styles)
Total number of logatomes	133,403
Utterances labeled as containing unwanted sounds	1,820
Number of utterances per dialect/accent	~2,700
Number of utterances per variability	~27,000
Number of utterances per central consonant	~4,450
Number of utterances per central vowel	~7,100

TABLE 2.1 *Properties of the OLLO speech database.*

(East Frisian dialect, EF), from East Phalia (EP) near Magdeburg, and from Bavarian places near Munich (BV). The French-speaking participants were recorded in Mons (Belgium). Five female and five male speakers from each region were recorded, resulting in a total of 50 speakers. The age of subjects varied between 18 and 65 years. Each logatome was recorded in 'neutral/clear' speaking style as a reference. In addition, one of the five selected variabilities (i.e., fast and slow speaking rate, loud and soft speaking style, and condition 'question' which refers to rising pitch) was alterered for each of the subsequent recordings. To provide a broad test and training basis for ASR experiments and to enable an analysis of intra-individual differences, each logatome was recorded three times which resulted in $150 \times (5+1) \times 3 = 2,700$ logatomes per speaker. Additionally, for German speakers 72 German words which are part of the monosyllabic rhyme test (Kollmeier and Wallenberg, 1989) and 20 German sentences part of the Goettingen sentence test (Kollmeier et al., 1997) were included. Participants from Belgium recorded 20 French sentences. This speech material is phonetically balanced and can be used for ASR speaker adaptation.

2.2.3 Recording setup

Technical equipment

All utterances were recorded in sound-insulated audiometry rooms (reverberation time: approx. 0.25 s) with a studio-quality condenser microphone (AKG C1000 S) placed approx. 30 cm from the speaker. Recordings were carried out using a RME QuadMic microphone pre-amplifier and an RME Hammerfall AD converter connected to a standard notebook. The software for the presentation of logatome transcriptions and for recording was based on Matlab (The MathWorks) and SoundMex (HoerTech GmbH). The original sampling frequency was 44.1 kHz at 32 bit resolution, which was reduced to 16 kHz and 16 bit during post processing.

Recording conditions

Since the database was intended to contain speech from phonetically naïve subjects, a transcription of the desired logatome and variability was created by a phonetician and presented to speakers on a computer screen (an example being 'Please speak ascha loudly', where 'ascha' is intepreted as /aʃa/ by German subjects). An adjustement of transcriptions was carried out for recordings of French speakers as well. Special attention was paid to the transcription and pronunciation of the near-closed phonemes /ɪ/ and /ʊ/ which are absent from French. Typographic accents and duration markers were used for the transcription. However, control samples showed that a considerable part of vowels embedded in CVCs is nevertheless categorized as closed phonemes /i/ and /u/ by linguists and the majority of German listeners. This is due to the fact that non-native speakers replace unfamiliar phonemes in the target language, which is absent in their native laguage phoneme inventory, with the sound considered as the closest in their native language phoneme inventory (Flege et al., 2003). This replacement is likely to increase errors for speakers with accent.

Randomized sequences of 150 logatomes with the same variability were recorded. After each run, a different variability was randomly chosen for the next sequence. Speakers were supervised during the recordings and periodically reminded to speak in the desired manner. All VCV stimuli were produced with front stress. During training sessions, speakers could familiarize themselves with the recording software which included proceeding to the next item by pressing a key on a keyboard and the option for re-recording of utterances that were contaminated with unwanted sounds or were not judged by the subject or the supervisor to be uttered in the appropriate way. Speakers were advised to speak in a natural manner; the realization of variabilities was checked and corrected if necessary. Some of the logatomes that contain a short vowel embedded in plosives (e.g. /p a p/) cannot be spoken slowly. Speakers were asked to articulate the logatome with normal speaking rate when the desired variability would conflict with the pronunciation. Participants were encouraged to take regular breaks to avoid mis-pronunciation due to inattentiveness. The average duration of the whole recording procedure was 3.5 hours per speaker.

2.2.4 Postprocessing of recorded material

A quality check of the recordings was carried out using a semi-automatic software written in Matlab which relied on a simple energy criterion to detect incomplete utterances or recordings with an audible keystroke. Unwanted sounds coinciding with the silence before or after the utterance were manually removed from the signal. 1,597 signals that were incomplete or had background noise in the speech signal were removed from the database. Another 1,820 utterances were labeled as containing a quiet, unwanted sound, which is audible in silence, but not in the presence of noise. The silence at the beginning and at the end of each recording was limited to 500 ms. Signals were then normalized to 99 % amplitude and stored with 16 bit resolution. They were low-pass filtered with 8 kHz cutoff frequency and sampled down to 16 kHz. Effects caused by these sounds are assumed to be negligible for these measurements, as subsets of OLLO database were chosen for listening tests, and unsuitable utterances were removed from those sets.

2.2.5 Phonetic labeling

The OLLO corpus was phonetically time-labeled, i.e., temporal positions of phoneme boundaries have been determined for each utterance, making it suitable for tasks such as training of phoneme recognizers. Labeling was performed with the 'Munich Automatic Segmentation System' (MAUS) software package provided by the Bavarian Archive for Speech Signals (BAS). The MAUS labeling procedure is similar to forced alignment approaches based on hidden Markov models (HMMs). However, in contrast to standard forced alignment, it has the ability to take into account pronunciation variations typical to a given language by computing a statistically weighted graph of all likely pronunciation variants. For details, the reader is referred to (Kipp et al., 1996).

All 150 logatomes were transcribed in the SAM phonetic alphabet (SAMPA) and the transcription was used as input for the time-labeling procedure. The MAUS labeling tool was applied to the data in 'full mode', i.e., taking into account pronunciation variations of the German language, and in addition the same software was applied in 'align-only' mode where HMM forced alignment is performed, but pronunciation variants are not considered.

In about 4.7 % of the logatomes, the MAUS method's result deviated from the forced alignment result. Most of these differences (75 %) can be accounted for by negligible shifts in phoneme boundary positions. The remaining quarter of the utterances with deviating boundaries had a pronunciation variant identified by MAUS. Most of such variations corresponded to shifts from short vowel forms (e.g., [a]) to the longer form (e.g., [a:]), which are plausible variations of the orthographic transcript presented to the subjects. The relative rarity of such variations indicates that in the vast majority of utterances the chosen orthographic transcript was pronounced in the way intended by the experimenters.

2.2.6 Availability of speech material and test results

The OLLO database, including a detailed description, wordlists, labeling files, technical specifications and calibration data (normalization coefficients and dB (SPL) values) is freely available for research in HSR and ASR. The uncompressed corpus is approx. 6.4 GB in size and contains a total of approximately 140,000 files corresponding to 60 hours of speech. It can be downloaded from http://medi.uni-oldenburg.de/ollo.

2.3 Methods

2.3.1 Test sets and presented stimuli

Utterances from the OLLO databases were selected to analyze the effects of speaking style and effort, dialect and accent, and SNR. These selections are referred to as sets, and their properties have been summarized in Table 2.2. Set V aims at differences

	Set V	Set D	Set S
Subject of test set	Speaking effort, rate and style	Dialect and accent	Signal-to-noise ratio
Speakers	S01M, S02F, S06M, S08F	S01M, S02F, S17M, S19F, S23F, S30M, S32M, S40F, S41F, S42M	S01M
Dialect / accent	No dialect	No dialect, East Frisian, Bavarian, East Phalian, French	No dialect
SNR (dB)	-6.2	-6.2	-20, -15, -10, -5, 0
Variability	Normal, fast, slow, soft, loud, question	Normal	Normal
Number of utterances	3,600	1,500	750
Number of listeners	6	6	10
Number of presentations	21,600	7,500	7,500

TABLE 2.2 *Subsets of the OLLO database used for human listening tests. The sets are used to analyze the influence of variabilities such as speaking rate and effort (Set V), dialect or accent (Set D) and SNR (Set S). Each set contains at least 150 different logatomes with 24 central phonemes which are subject of listening experiments. The supplements 'F' and 'M' in row 'speakers' correspond to female and male talkers, respectively. For sets with more than one speaker, the gender is equally distributed.*

caused by speaking rate, effort, and style. It contains data from four speakers (two male, two female) without regional dialect (ND = no dialect) with six variabilities. Set D contains utterances from two speakers (one male, one female) from each of the five dialect/accent regions with normal speaking style. From the 50 speakers in the database, those speakers were chosen as being representative for the corpus that produced recognition rates for a standard automatic speech recognition task which were closest to the average recognition rate: Standard ASR features (i.e., mel-frequency cepstral coefficients with delta and acceleration features) were used as input for a hidden Markov model (HMM). The HMM was trained with utterances from 49 speakers and was subsequently tested with logatomes from the remaining speaker. This procedure was performed for all speakers in the corpus, and the results were used to compile subsets that yield similar overall performance as the complete set of speakers.

When presented without masking noise, human phoneme recognition scores were found to be very close to 100 %. In a phoneme recognition task with clean speech signals, the lowest recognition rate was found to be 95 % in the presence of variabilities (Meyer et al., 2006). This high performance prevents a valid analysis of phoneme confusions, because differences at very high error rates often are outside the range of reliably observable differences (ceiling effect). Hence, speech-shaped noise is used to increase the difficulty of the listening task (cf. Section 2.3.3). A fixed SNR of -6.2 dB for Sets V and D was chosen based on pilot measurements with the goal of producing recognition rates of 70 to 80 % in average.

For Set S, the utterances of one speaker (no dialect) and normal speaking style were used to analyze the dependency of recognition performance and noise. Speech-weighted noise at signal-to-noise ratios ranging from -20 dB to 0 dB was added to the logatomes. A summary of the test subsets V, D and S is listed in Table 2.2.

2.3.2 Measurement setup and listeners

Sixteen German, normal-hearing listeners (10M, 6F) without regional dialect (cf. Section 2.2.6) participated in the HSR tests. From those sixteen subjects, six listeners (three male, three female) participated in the measurements with Set V. Of those six, five listeners (three male, two female) also participated in the measurements of Set D. Ten other subjects (7 male, 3 female) were chosen for Set S. The listeners were between 18 and 38 years old. Their hearing threshold for pure tones in standard audiometry did not exceed +20 dB at more than one data point and +10 dB at more than two data points in the pure tone audiogram. Randomized sequences of logatomes were presented in a soundproof booth and via audiological headphones (Sennheiser HDA200) after an online free-field equalization was performed. Feedback or the possibility to replay the logatome was not given during the test procedure. After a training phase, subjects were presented a sequence of logatomes at a level of 70 dB SPL. For each presentation, a logatome had to be selected from a randomized list of CVCs or VCVs with the same outer phoneme and different middle phonemes. A computer mouse was used as input device. In order to avoid errors due to inattentiveness, listeners were encouraged to take regular breaks. The total measurement time for each listener varied between six and nine hours, including pauses and instructions for listeners. It was distributed across different days (including a daily training session prior to data recording) in order not to exceed three hours of measurement for each day and each subject.

2.3.3 Noise and SNR calculation

A stationary noise signal with speech-like frequency characteristics was chosen as masker for the logatomes (Dreschler et al. (2001); http://www.icra.nu). It was introduced by the International Collegium of Rehabilitative Audiology (ICRA) and implemented by adding artificial speech signals that represented a single speaker speaking with normal effort. The spectral and temporal properties were controlled and had a close resemblance to real-life communication without clear modulation, equivalent to a situation with loud cocktail party noise.

The original ICRA1 noise was downsampled from 44.1 kHz to 16 kHz using the Matlab resample function. The average DFT power spectrum of the resampled noise signal is shown in Fig. 2.1. It exhibits a constant power between 100 and 500 Hz, and a constant roll-off of 9.1 dB/oct between 500 Hz and 19 kHz.

Fig. 2.1 shows the long-term spectra of logatomes with different central phonemes. The long-term spectra were obtained by calculating the rms (root mean square) average of the 1024-point FFTs of each utterance. The mean spectra were normalized to have the same rms level before plotting. By using this calculation scheme, the spectral properties of both vowels and consonants are represented in the long-term spectrum. However, since for each central vowel the type and number of outer consonants is the same (and vice versa), the effects of outer phonemes are expected to average out.

For such short utterances as logatomes, the adjustment and interpretation of the SNR is not a trivial issue because the short-term level derived from each logatome varies considerably across logatomes even if exactly the same recording conditions are

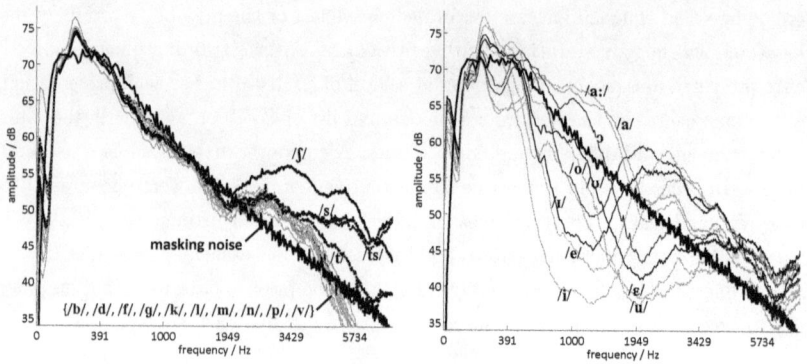

FIG. 2.1 *Average DFT power spectrum of stationary masking noise signal (thick black line) and long-term spectra of OLLO utterances. Individual long-term spectra for central consonant and vowel phonemes are shown in the left and right panel, respectively. Mel-scaling with labels in Hz has been chosen for the frequency axis.*

used (i.e., technical conditions, speaker, speech rate, speech effort,...). Obviously, the reliability of the short-term level as an estimate of the "true" speech level decreases with decreasing duration of the speech segment. One option for a more valid speech level measure as an input to the SNR measure would therefore be to use the *average* power of all speech samples in the database, since the long-term SNR has been shown by the Articulation Index and the Speech Intelligibility Index to be a reliable measure for *average* speech intelligibility. By using such a long-term speech level, changes in the recording conditions (e.g., variations of the distance between speaker and microphone) can be reliably detected and compensated for. On the other hand, the short-term rms level of a *single* utterance is an easily computable local measure that does not rely on the (statistical) properties of the remaining speech corpus and captures best the properties of the individual speech item. Hence, the short-term SNR is very popular in speech research and has been used, e.g., in other studies that make use of CV utterances in noise (as, e.g., Phatak and Allen (2007)). However, due to the large statistical uncertainty with short speech segments, the intelligibility obtained from short VCV and CVC combinations varies considerably across speech items in a way not predictable from the variability of the short-term SNR and only partially predictable from the long-term SNR (Kollmeier, 1990) which compensates for slow variations of the recording conditions. Since these variations were already controlled and compensated for during the recording of the OLLO speech corpus and for the sake of simplicity and compatibility with recent studies, we used the short-term SNR derived from each single utterance throughout this study.

For measurements with Sets D and S, the SNR was calculated by relating the root-mean-square value of the speech segments of each audio signal and the rms value of a masking noise of equal length. A simple voice detection algorithm based on an energy criterion was used to extract connected speech segments. Random control samples were chosen to control proper functioning of that algorithm. For utterances from Set V, a different SNR calculation scheme was applied: In this case, the rms levels of the whole utterance (including silence) and a noise segment of equal length were used to adjust the SNR. Since the length of silence before and after each logatome is 500 ms and because the variation of temporal spread of identical logatomes is relatively small, this corresponds to a fixed offset which was found to be 3.8 dB compared to the SNR calculation scheme mentioned above. For clarity, the SNR values for Set V are converted to the first mentioned method.

2.3.4 Data analysis

Confusions matrices

A detailed analysis of the outcome of listening experiments is presented in terms of confusion matrices (CMs). CMs characterize how often a presented phoneme was correctly classified or confused with a response alternative. The rows correspond to *presented* phonemes and the columns correspond to *recognized* items. CMs are normalized and rounded, so that each row adds up to approx. 100 %.

Articulatory features

The acoustic cues important for consonant identification are analyzed by decomposing consonants into their articulatory features. This method of data analysis is based on works by Miller and Nicely (1955) who proposed five linguistic or articulatory features to group speech stimuli, i.e., voicing, nasality, affriction, duration, place of articulation. The features of nasality and affriction may be combined into one feature 'manner of articulation' with three possible feature values (stop, nasal or fricative) which refers to

Consonant	p	t	k	b	d	g	s	f	v	n	m
Voicing	0	0	0	1	1	1	0	0	1	1	1
Manner	0	0	0	0	0	0	1	1	1	2	2
Place	0	1	2	0	1	2	1	0	0	1	0

TABLE 2.3 *Articulatory features for the 11 consonants used for the data analysis. Voicing is a binary feature (feature values 1 = voiced, 0 = unvoiced), while the other features have three possibly features values (Manner: 0 = stop, 1 = fricative, 2 = nasal; place: 0 = anterior, 1 = medial, 2 = posterior).*

the mode of articulatory production. For this study, we present an exemplary analysis including the features voicing, manner, and place of articulation, with values as shown in Table 2.3. The analysis is based on consonants. The phonemes /l/, /ʃ/ and /ts/ were excluded because they would have required the introduction of new feature values for which only few representatives exist.

Values in the articulatory CM do not solely depend on the information transmission associated with a particular feature and stimulus condition but also on the entropy of the respective feature. This feature entropy may change even if no information has been transmitted for example if any response bias occurs or if the distribution of the chance performance is changed by any other means. To correct for this effect, the amount of transmitted information was computed by measuring the relationship between a specific stimulus x and the response categories y without the influence of any possible response bias. The information transmission (or mutual information) is computed using the expression

$$T(x,y) = -\sum_{i,j} p_{ij} \log \frac{p_i p_j}{p_{ij}} \qquad (2.1)$$

with the input variable x and the output variable y, each having the possible values $i = 1, 2, \ldots, k$ and $j = 1, 2, \ldots, m$, respectively, with the corresponding probabilities p_i, p_j, and the joint probability p_{ij}. The indices i and j refer to the index of the corresponding feature as listed in Table 2.3, or to the consonant index, respectively. The probabilities p_i and p_j are the *a-priori* and *a-posteriori* probabilities for the stimuli, while p_{ij} is a matrix element of the confusion matrix, either of the consonant confusions or the derived matrices for articulatory features. This method can be used to obtain the information transmission for each phonetic feature (voicing, manner, and place) by determining $T(x,y)$ from the confusion matrices for the phonetic features. Since the logarithm is taken to the base 2, $T(x,y)$ is a measure of how many bits are required to specify the input. To compare transmitted information from distinct features, we report the relative information transmission $T_r(x, y) = T(x, y)/H(x)$ with the source entropy $H(x) = \sum_i p_i \log(p_i)$ throughout this study (Miller and Nicely, 1955).

Spectral distance

Differences in recognition rate may be caused by spectral, temporal or spectro-temporal cues that are associated with the according phoneme. We analyze the spectral effects based on a simple measure of level distance $D(X_i,N)$ between phoneme and masking spectrum:

$$D(X_i, N) = \frac{1}{M} \sum_{f,X_i(f)>N(f)+10 \ dB}^{M} (X_i(f) - N(f))^2 \qquad (2.2)$$

where $X_i(f)$ is the long-term frequency spectrum of the ith central phoneme, $N(f)$ is the masking frequency spectrum and M is the number of samples of X_i. To account for the higher critical bandwidth towards higher frequencies in the human auditory system, the long-term spectra are grouped in 45 mel-frequency bins and converted to a dB-scale before calculating the difference between signal and noise. Therefore, level and frequency perception of the human auditory system is approximated, so that the spectral level distance can be seen as a very coarse model for the psycho-physical distance of sounds. The calculation of spectra is described in Section 2.3.3. The level of the masking spectrum is raised by 10 dB before the parts of the signal above noise level are used to calculate $D(X_i,N)$. This procedure is similar to the calculation of the articulation index (French and Steinberg, 1947) where the dynamic range of speech sounds (i.e., approx. 30 dB) is adjusted to the mean noise level so that the information-carrying peak energy portions of speech are adjusted to the average noise level.

A second parameter that is likely to influence recognition is the spectral dissimilarity to other *phonemes*. Analogous to Equation 2.2, we define the distance between the long-term spectra X_i and X_j of the ith and jth phoneme as

$$D(X_i, X_j) = \frac{1}{M} \sum_f^M (X_i(f) - X_j(f))^2. \hspace{2cm} (2.3)$$

By relating those differences to recognition results or error rates, the effect of such dissimilarities can be quantified.

2.4 Results

2.4.1 Overall recognition scores

Overall recognition accuracies are reported for test Sets V, D and S in Fig. 2.2. Scores

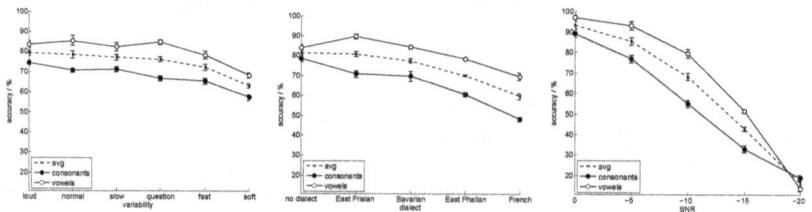

FIG. 2.2 *Phoneme recognition results (% correct) with standard errors, depending on speech-intrinsic variabilities such as speaking rate and style (Set V, left panel) and dialect (Set D, middle panel), and on additive masking noise (right panel). Results for Sets V and D were obtained in listening experiments at -6.2 dB SNR in speech-shaped noise. Variabilities are sorted by average recognition accuracies which are broken down into consonant and vowel scores.*

are broken down into consonant/vowel recognition and the varied parameter. For Sets V and D, the overall recognition rate is about 74 %, with large differences between consonants and vowels, the latter producing far better accuracies at this masking level of -6.2 dB.

Recognition scores depending on speech-intrinsic variabilities obtained with Set V are shown in the left panel of Fig. 2.2. Best overall results are obtained for high speaking effort (condition 'loud', 79.3 %) and the reference condition (78.6 %). The variabilities 'slow' and 'question' result in medium accuracies (rel. increase of WER:

10.1 and 14.5 %), while the increase of WER is considerably higher for the variabilities
'fast' and 'slow' (33.8 % and 77.3 %, respectively).

For measurements with varied dialect (Fig. 2.2, middle panel), the reference condition
('no dialect') produces the highest intelligibility (81.5 %), as expected for this group of
listeners that came from a region without any strong accent. It is interesting to note
that East Frisian dialect (EF) results in higher vowel accuracy than speech without
dialect. An analysis of the CM for vowels from EF speakers showed that listeners
learned to recognize the distinct pronunciation of mid and open vowels. French accent
results in lowest intelligibility (59.7 %), both for consonant and vowel recognition.
Even if problematic phonemes that are absent from French are excluded from the
analysis, the scores are still below the performance of other conditions. SNR-dependent
recognition performance is shown in the right panel of Fig. 2.2. Vowel accuracies are
consistently higher than those of consonants, with the exception of the lowest SNR
(-20 dB) which is presumably a result of ceiling effects.

2.4.2 Effects of additive noise and intrinsic variabilities

Since all measurements are based on the same speech corpus, effects of variability
changes obtained with Sets V and D can be expressed in terms of differences of the
signal-to-noise ratio that were measured with Set S. This is shown in Fig. 2.3 where
the accuracies for Sets V and D are projected on the SNR dependent recognition scores.
The projection of variability-dependent scores shows that an average performance
corresponds to an SNR of 12.2 dB. The accuracy for the normal speaking style is higher
and corresponds to an SNR of 10.8 dB, resulting in a SNR difference of 1.4 dB. In case
of varied dialect or accent, the SNR shift amounts to 2.7 dB. If accuracies obtained
with French speech are excluded from this comparison (due to phonetic dissimilarities
in German/English vs. French), the gap reduces to 1.5 dB SNR.

Since the recognition setup implied a closed test where the outer phonemes of choice
alternatives are the same for each presentation, no confusions occur between VCVs
and CVCs. Therefore, separate CMs are shown for consonant and vowel confusions
(Table 2.4 and Table 2.5, respectively). Results show that the spread in accuracy is
larger for consonants (with scores ranging from 36 to 99 %) while vowel recognition
is more robust in general (72 to 90 %). Highest consonant scores were obtained for
the phoneme group (/t/, /s/, /ʃ/, /ts/, /f/) which is in accordance with observations

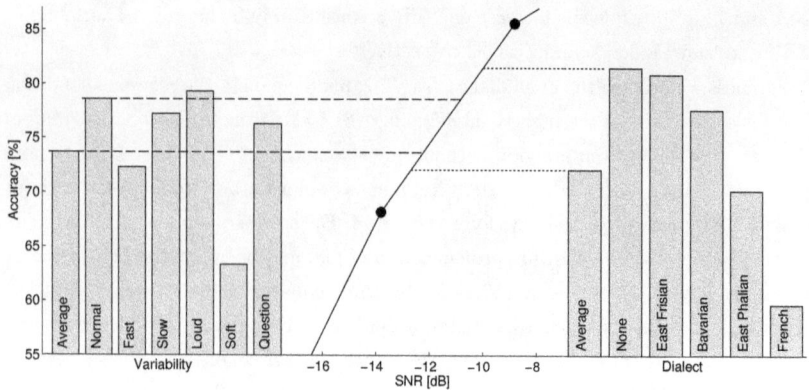

FIG. 2.3 *Average recognition rates depending on speaking variability (left panel), SNR (middle panel) and dialect or accent (right panel). The dashed horizontal lines show the difference between logatomes in the 'normal' condition and the average performance of the remaining variabilities. Dotted lines denote differences between the 'no dialect' condition and the remaining dialects. By projecting these differences on the middle panel, changes in speaking variability may be expressed in terms of SNR.*

from Phatak and Allen (2007) who found similar results for the high-scoring consonant phonemes /t/, /s/, /z/, /ʃ/ and /ʒ/. In Table 2.1, the highest error rates are observed for /a/ and /aː/ which was expected due to their phonetic similarity, as discussed in Section 2.2, and their spectral similarity which can be seen from Fig. 2.1.

2.4.3 Influence of spectral differences

The dissimilarities between long-term spectra of high-scoring fricatives and the masking noise (Fig. 2.1) suggest that spectral properties of phonemes might be a good predictor for the observed differences of recognition rates. The distance between phoneme and masking spectrum $D(X_i,N)$ was calculated according to Equation 2.1 and compared to recognition rates, as shown in Fig. 2.4 (left panel). In order to analyze the effect of dissimilarities between *pairs of phoneme spectra*, the spectral inter-phoneme level distance $D(X_i,X_j)$ is compared to *error rates* from CMs. Since $D(X_i,X_j)$ is a symmetric measure (i.e. $D(X_i, X_j) = D(X_j, X_i)$), confusion matrices C were symmetrized by

	p	t	k	b	d	g	s	f	v	n	m	ʃ	ts	l
p	52.6	2.8	18.2	6.3	1.0	4.3		6.8	6.4	0.6	0.7			0.4
t	0.4	91.4	2.2		4.6			0.1	0.1				1.0	0.1
k	5.8	1.9	67.2	1.4	1.1	16.3	0.1	2.2	1.7	0.8				1.4
b	8.1	0.6	7.1	36.1	4.9	12.2		2.5	19.9	2.2	3.5		0.1	2.9
d	0.7	3.9	1.0	2.9	58.9	12.9	0.1	0.4	2.6	6.8	0.8			8.9
g	1.5	0.7	6.1	6.0	3.8	62.4		1.3	10.1	2.5	1.0			4.7
s		0.3					97.5	0.4				0.8	1.0	
f	3.2		0.4	0.6			12.2	77.2	5.3			0.6	0.4	0.1
v	2.6	1.0	2.2	10.8	3.1	6.0	1.0	7.1	55.3	1.3	4.2		0.3	5.3
n	0.1	0.7	0.4	1.8	7.1	1.7		0.3	3.2	50.6	10.8			23.3
m	1.0	0.1	0.6	6.0	2.8	3.5		1.1	8.6	13.2	48.1			15.1
ʃ	0.1	0.6	0.1		0.1		0.3				0.1	98.5	0.1	
ts	0.1	10.0					3.6					0.1	86.1	
l	0.1	0.7	0.7	0.8	6.9	3.8		0.8	3.3	12.1	4.7	0.4		65.6
Sum	76.3	114.7	106.2	72.7	94.2	123.2	114.8	100.2	116.5	90.2	73.8	100.4	89.0	127.8

TABLE 2.4 *Confusion matrix for consonant phonemes obtained with Set V, pooled over all variabilities, listeners and speakers in this test set. The average recognition rate is 67.7%. Rows are normalized, with 100% corresponding to 720 presentations.*

$C_{sym} = \frac{1}{2}(C + C^T)$. The dependency of $D(X_i, X_j)$ of the corresponding error rate is shown in Fig. 2.4 (right panel).

A multi-dimensional analysis of variance (ANOVA) was applied to model the recognition scores and error rates as a function of the parameters $D(X_i, N)$, $D(X_i, X_j)$, and the phoneme type (consonant or vowel phoneme). The latter was included because large differences between the long-term spectra of vowels were observed (cf. Fig. 2.1), while consonant spectra exhibit only small differences over a large frequency range. It was investigated if this results in systematic differences between the phoneme types. Any significant correlation between recognition rates (and/or error rates, respectively) and physical parameter provides evidence for the underlying perception mechanism without necessarily establishing a causality relation.

The analysis for *error rates* was limited to confusions to phonemes that were spectrally closest to the presented phoneme. This was done for two reasons: First, confusions among phonemes with a high spectral distance did rarely occur, resulting in a flooring effect which suggested to consider only the phonemes which are spectrally closest to the presented phoneme. Second, by selecting the error rates of the nearest 'spectral

	a	aː	ɛ	e	ɪ	i	ɔ	o	ʊ	u
a	79.7	19.0	0.1				0.9		0.3	0.1
aː	15.5	83.6					0.2		0.2	0.6
ɛ	0.3		77.6	12.0	8.2	0.4		0.2	0.4	0.9
e			1.6	72.0	15.1	9.7		0.7	0.4	0.5
ɪ			2.4	8.4	86.2	1.3		0.5	0.9	0.3
i				2.3	6.1	90.4			0.3	1.0
ɔ	1.9	1.2					84.4	7.4	4.3	0.9
o			0.1	0.5	0.7	0.2	0.8	71.6	10.7	15.5
ʊ			0.3		1.3	0.1	2.0	11.7	77.9	6.7
u	0.1	0.1	0.1	0.1	1.0	2.4		7.6	6.9	81.6
Sum	97.5	103.9	82.2	95.3	118.6	104.5	88.3	99.7	102.3	108.1

TABLE 2.5 *CM for vowel phonemes, obtained with Set V. The average recognition rate is 80.5 %. For a detailed description, see Table 2.4.*

neighbor', the dimensionality of observations matched the number of parameters which is required for the ANOVA. In the following, the distance associated with the spectrally closest phoneme with index C1 will be referred to as $D(X_i,X_{C1})$ (and $D(X_i,X_{C2})$, $D(X_i,X_{C3})$ for the second and third closest phoneme, respectively). In all cases, 24 observations (corresponding to the 24 phoneme classes in OLLO) were used as input to the ANOVA.

The recognition rate $C(i,i)$ (i.e., the observed variable) was found to be significantly related to the distance to noise $D(X_i,N)$ ($p < 0.05$), whereas the phoneme-phoneme distance $D(X_i,X_{C1})$ and phoneme type had no significant effect. On the other hand, the observed *error rates* for the spectrally closest phoneme *C1* were affected by the distance $D(X_{C1},N)$, the phoneme type (both at the 5 % level of significance) and $D(X_i,X_{C1})$ ($p < 0.01$). Similarly, the confusions with the 2nd closest phoneme were influenced by $D(X_i,N)$, $D(X_i,X_{C2})$, and phoneme type (all at the 1 % level of significance). An interaction was found for the two distance measures $D(X_i,N)$ and $D(X_i,X_j)$ ($p < 0.05$) which is plausible since a speech-shaped noise was used as masker, and the average phoneme exhibits a spectrum similar to this masker. However, these effects were not consistently observed for 'more distant phonemes' (i.e., phonemes that were more separated than the second nearest neighbor). This is presumably due to the fact that phonemes are not confused when a certain threshold of dissimilarity is exceeded (which results in a flooring effect as mentioned above). When using all error rates as observed

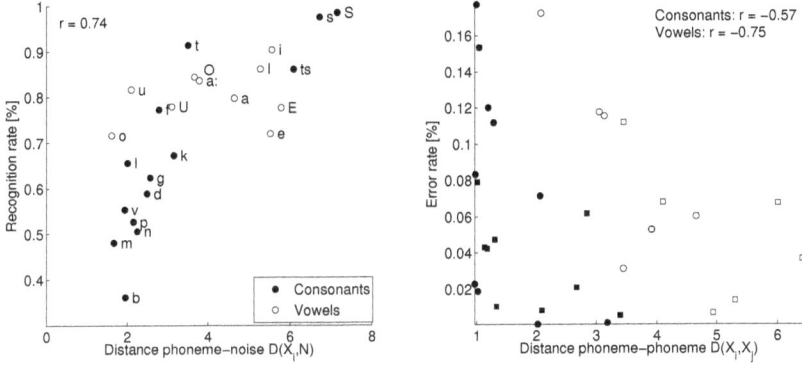

FIG. 2.4 *Left panel: Relation between the phoneme-noise distance and recognition rates for consonants and vowels. Next to each data point, the SAMPA transcript of the according phoneme is denoted. The right panel shows the dependency of phoneme-phoneme distance and error rates obtained from symmetrized confusion matrices. For each phoneme, several data points are shown which correspond to confusions with 'spectral neighbours', i.e., phonemes that were spectrally closest (marker $\circ$), 2nd and 3rd closest (markers $\square$ and $\diamond$, respectively) to the presented phoneme.*

quantity, the phoneme-phoneme distance ($p < 0.01$) and phoneme class ($p < 0.05$) were found to have a significant effect.

In Fig. 2.4, the relation between recognition and error rates, respectively and the spectral distances are given as a scatter plot together with a correlation coefficient. Since the results of the ANOVA suggested that the distinction between consonant and vowel phonemes does not significantly affect recognition rates, we report the correlation for all phonemes ($r = 0.74$, $p < 0.01$). Phoneme *confusions* were however shown to be influenced by the phoneme type. The dependency of error rates and the distance to phonemes which are spectrally close was found to be stronger for vowels ($r = -0.75$, $p < 0.01$) than for consonants ($r = -0.57$, $p < 0.01$). When including both phoneme types in the analysis, this dependency is somewhat degraded, but still significant ($r = -0.31$, $p < 0.05$).

The very simple measure of spectral phoneme-masker and inter-phoneme differences fails to explain for all the observed recognition and error rates of human listeners. An improved prediction requires models that are based on human principles of auditory processing, e.g., the extraction of spectro-temporal features that exhibit a higher signal-to-noise ratio in an appropriate "glimpse" of the time-frequency distribution (Kleinschmidt and Gelbart, 2002; Barker and Cooke, 2007).

2.4.4 Articulatory features and information transmission

The overall results (Fig. 2.2) showed that speech-intrinsic variabilities induce strong differences in performance for the chosen signal-to-noise ratio. The transmitted information of articulatory features is analyzed in order to pinpoint those cues that are most strongly affected in the presence of variabilities. The information channels under consideration were voicing, manner, and place of articulation. These features are well-defined for consonant phonemes, for which the analysis is performed by deriving confusion matrices for articulatory features from the consonant CMs for each variability. These matrices were used to calculate T_r scores, as described in Section 2.3.4. Relative information transmission scores T_r depending on speaking effort, rate and dialect are shown in Fig. 2.5.

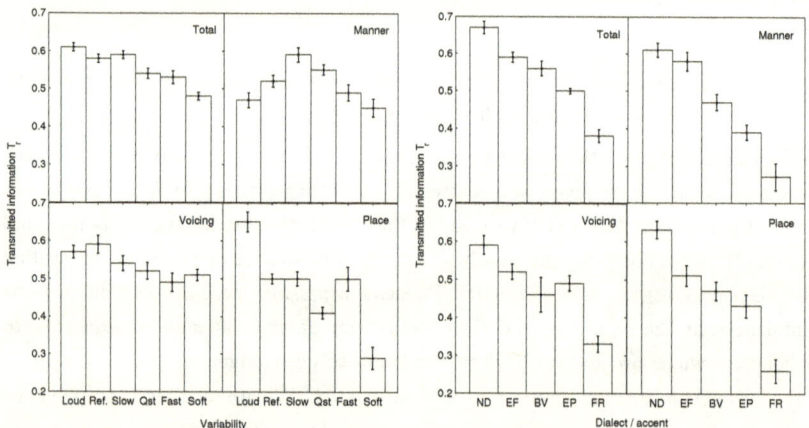

FIG. 2.5 *Relative information transmission T_r depending on speaking variability such as speaking rate and effort (left panel) and dialect and accent (right panel) for selected articulatory features. The error bars denote the standard error across listeners.*

An analysis of variance was performed using the T_r-scores obtained with Set V for each of the articulatory features and by using the explanatory parameters 'speaker', 'listener' and 'speaking style, rate or effort'. This resulted in 4 (no. of speakers) × 6 (no. of listeners) × 6 (no. of variabilities) observations for each of the AFs. The choice of speaker had a strong effect on the transmitted information ($p < 0.01$ for all AFs). Effects of subject and speaking variability on the relative transmitted information were found for manner and place of articulation ($p < 0.01$) but not for the voicing feature ($p = 0.11$). Furthermore, we observed strong interactions between speaker and variability, but no interactions between listeners and speakers, or listeners and intrinsic variability.

Soft speaking style produced the lowest overall transmission scores, which complies with the consonant results reported in Fig. 2.2. A major difference compared to the reference condition are high error rates for /p/ and /b/ and confusions between the nasals /n/ and /m/. The latter seems to be the major reason for the low scores of the place feature in soft speaking style (0.29). In contrast to this, place is well recognized for loud speaking style (0.65), with a higher T_r score than normal speaking style (0.50). An analysis of CMs for the place feature showed that this is mainly caused by reduced confusions between anterior and medial placed constrictions of the vocal tract, reflecting overarticulation of loudly spoken utterances.

Slow speaking rate exhibits above average scores for all features. The manner of articulation is particularly well recognized in this case, with a relative increase of 13 % of transmitted information, compared to the reference condition. Voicing shows only small variations of T_r scores, which range from 49 to 59 %, and was not found to be significantly influenced by speaking style and rate. This AF therefore appears as being relatively robust towards the discussed variations.

A second ANOVA was carried out, with the transmitted information for each AF derived from measurements with Set D as observed variable. The choice of speaker, listener and the dialect were included as explanatory parameters. This resulted in 10 (speaker) × 5 (listener) observations. Since chosing a certain speaker also specifies the dialect/accent, the number of dialects does not increase the number of observations. Dialect and accent and the choice of speaker had a significant influence on the articulatory features ($p < 0.01$), whereas the choice of listener had not. Relative information transmission depending on dialect and accent is shown in Fig. 2.5 (right panel). Not surprisingly, the highest values for all features are obtained for standard German. Compared to this, transmitted information for all features is approx. halved for French-accented speech, while the scores for German dialects are in between those conditions. Speech with dialect/accent exhibits the highest relative degradation of information associated with place of articulation. This specific degradation of the place feature is consistent with the notion that the dialects employed differ primarily with respect to the place of articulation. The articulation of voicing and manner, on the other hand, seem to be more constrained by language-specific rules, which results in less variation in transmitted information.

The feature 'manner' is relatively well transmitted for East Frisian dialect, due to reduced confusions between plosives and fricatives. For example, the error rates for the confusion between /v/ and /b/ is almost halved. In case of East Phalian dialect, the voicing feature has relatively high values, as confusions between voiced-unvoiced pairs such as /b/,/p/ are reduced.

2.5 Discussion

In this study we presented results from speech intelligibility tests with the OLLO logatome speech database that covers several speech-intrinsic variabilities. From the wide range of variations of spoken language, we chose those that were found to severely degrade performance of automatic recognizers. A speech-shaped masking noise was used to avoid ceiling effects in phoneme recognition. Soft and fast speaking style were identified as the most problematic for human listeners, as relative error rates increased by approx. 70 and 30 %, respectively, compared to the reference condition. The other variabilities (reduced rate of speech, increased speaking effort and rising pitch) influenced global recognition scores to a lesser extent (i.e., between 3 % and 11 %), but resulted in shifts of microscopic phoneme confusions.

The presented experiments are limited to a selection of variabilities that were either documented or systematically varied during the recordings of the database. Future experiments may also take other sources of variation into account, such as the effects of age, coarticulation and gender, which has been shown to be a major factor for variations of spoken language (Hazan and Markham, 2004).

2.5.1 Comparison with past work

A comparison with important studies on consonant recognition is presented in Fig. 2.6. It includes data from Phatak and Allen (2007) [PA07], Grant and Walden (1996) [GW96]

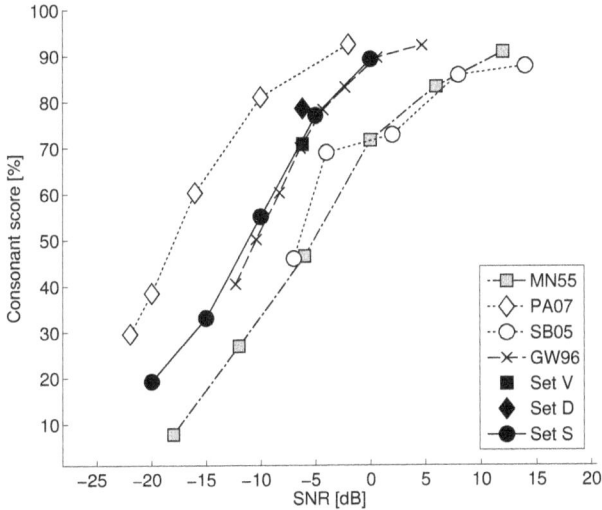

FIG. 2.6 *Comparison of average consonant recognition scores with results from Sroka and Braida (2005) [SB05], Phatak and Allen (2007) [PA07], Grant and Walden (1996) [GW96], and Miller and Nicely (1955) [MN55]. Filled symbols denote results obtained with the OLLO database. Recognition scores for Sets V and D for 'normal' speaking style and 'no dialect' condition include a single SNR and appear as single data points.*

and Sroka and Braida (2005) [SB05], all of which measured consonant recognition scores in speech-shaped noise. Results from Miller and Nicely (1955) [MN55] who used white noise as masker are also shown. The results obtained in five studies (including the current paper) form three groups with respect to average consonant identification scores: Scores from GW96 and from Sets V, D and S show good resemblance; the performance obtained in these experiments is between PA07 (for which the performance is 20 % higher in average) and SB05 and MN55 (for which it is 20 % lower). The highest spread in average recognition performance for sounds masked with speech-shaped noise is observed between PA07 and SB05 with an absolute difference of 39 %. Since the slope of the performance-intensity curves for all data given in Figure 2.6 is almost identical for 50 % consonant intelligibility ($\sim$4.5 %/ dB), the observed difference can be expressed in terms of the SNR: Using a linear interpolation for the mid-region of the performance-intensity curves shown in Fig. 2.6, the SNR shift was determined which resulted in the smallest rms error between the shifted data from the literature and the scores obtained in this study (Set S). While this shift was very small for the GW96 data (0.5 dB), the differences for the other studies are more noticeable (PA07: -6.5 dB; SB05: +5 dB; MN55: +6 dB).

There are numerous reasons for the observed variations across studies: Since the spectral differences between phoneme and masker is of primary importance for the phoneme recognition rate (cf. Section 2.4.3), a major part of the observed variations can be predicted using a simple approach based on the spectral level difference to compensate for the effect of spectral masker and phoneme properties on recognition scores and error rates. The results are in line with findings from PA07 where a modified version of the articulation index (AI) with frequency-dependent weighting coefficients was used, which resulted in a close match of data from MN55, PA07, and GW97. However, the close resemblance of scores between MN55 and SB05 (where masking noises with different characteristics were employed) or the large SNR-shift between PA07 and SB05 (both of which used a speech-shaped masking noise) suggests that average spectral differences are not sufficient as the only important factor in phoneme recognition. Hence, other experimental parameters have to be considered that differ across the studies under consideration: The number of consonant phonemes lies between 12 (SB05) and 18 (GW96). This number influences both chance performance as well as any phoneme confusions that depend on the similarity of phonemes, which affects overall error rates. Furthermore, coarticulation effects presumably affect the results, as the number of vowels paired with the consonant lies between one (MN55) and five (this work). The difference in SNR calculation might also contribute to the observed shift, as mentioned in Section 2.3.3.

Recognition scores depending on speaking rate and style are consistent with other studies. Krause and Braida (2002) presented experiments with conversational and clear speech (i.e., speech with higher intelligibility than conversational speech) with different speaking rates and styles. In our study, we confirm the finding that loudly spoken utterances result in highest intelligibility (after compensating for different absolute speech levels), followed by slow, fast and soft speaking style (in that order). The absolute differences of recognition scores reported by Krause and Braida (2002) are larger than found in this study, i.e. the difference between loud and soft speaking style amounts to 27 percentage-points in Krause and Braida (2002) and to 16 percentage-points in this study. For this comparison we refer to results obtained with conversational speech in Krause and Braida (2002), rather than clear speech that was produced by trained speakers, since speakers recorded for the OLLO database were encouraged to speak in normal or natural way. However, this larger difference in speech intelligibility score across studies can be explained by the presumably steeper performance-intensity curve for Krause and Braida (2002) where listeners had to identify key words from sentences, in comparison to the flat curve for phonemes employed here ($\sim$4.5 %/ dB, see above). Another factor that significantly influences intelligibility is the inter-individual difference of talkers. Krause and Braida (2003) have shown that two talkers who were trained to produce clear speech at normal speaking rates employed very different strategies for performing this task. For example, large differences of acoustic properties such as voice-onset time and the duration and extent of formant transitions were observed for the talkers. This result underlines the difficulties that arise when results obtained with different speakers are compared, especially when variabilities of speech are considered in connection with unnatural articulation modes (such as, speaking "loud" or "clear") where stronger changes due to additional variations (e.g., speaking rate or style) are expected than in normal speech. In this work, we tried to control for these differences by recording several variabilities from the same set of speakers.

2.5.2 Comparison between HSR and ASR

In other studies the OLLO corpus has been successfully applied to the problem of ASR (Wesker et al., 2005; Meyer et al., 2007), as an evaluation tool for speech models (Jürgens et al., 2007) and to study speaker discrimination of patients (Mühler et al., 2009). By making the speech corpus available for research in HSR and ASR, we hope to promote research dealing with the impact of speech-intrinsic variabilities on both human and automatic recognition. The HSR scores presented in this study may serve as baseline for experiments that aim at narrowing the gap between ASR and HSR, which is still one of the most important challenges in speech research. The speech database, measurement results and detailed results from the analysis can be obtained at http://medi.uni-oldenburg.de/ollo for research purposes.

An open question is if the results that were obtained with VCV and CVC utterances are scalable to continuously and conversational speech. Variations in conversational speech are considerable larger then recordings under controlled situations, as speaking rate and effort are subject to frequent changes. However, experiments comparable with our approach would require a database with labeled phonemes and variabilities, which does not yet exist to our knowledge. For the creation of suitable databases, problems such as the ambiguous labeling of phonemes are further aggravated in the presence of strong variations in spoken language, as, e.g., (Shriberg et al., 1984) have shown for transcription of children speech.

By relating recognition scores obtained for different variabilities and various SNRs, effects of changed speaking style were expressed in terms of SNR changes. Naturally, these results are valid for medium speech intelligibility only, as for very high SNRs a degradation of 2 dB will have a minor impact on performance, while stronger degradations are obtained when speaking style or dialect are varied (Meyer et al., 2006).

In future research, the impact of intrinsic variations on automatic speech recognition will be assessed and compared to the results obtained with human listening experiments. Such a comparison has been performed earlier (Lippmann, 1997; Sroka and Braida, 2005; Ten Bosch and Kirchhoff, 2007; Cooke and Scharenborg, 2008) with the aim of quantifying the gap between HSR and ASR, and the ultimate goal of bridging this gap (i.e., improving ASR) by employing principles that are at work in the human auditory system. While in other studies the focus was laid on extrinsic factors that severely degrade ASR (such as, e.g., the influence of cut-off frequencies of high- and lowpass filtered maskers or the non-stationarity of masking noises) we hope to highlight weaknesses of current ASR systems when speech with intrinsic variations represented in the OLLO speech corpus is to be recognized. The results may then be used to improve the robustness of ASR systems against such variations.

2.6 Summary & conclusions

The most important conclusions from this work can be summarized as follows:

1. The Oldenburg Logatome speech corpus (OLLO) was introduced, and results from human listening tests were reported in terms of error rates and transmission rates of characteristic speech features. The database consists of simple VCV and CVC utterances and covers several speech-intrinsic variabilities. It is available for research purposes with human and automatic speech recognition.

2. Speech-intrinsic variabilities such as speaking rate and style, intonation, and dialect affect the recognition performance of human listeners. High speaking effort produces increased intelligibility and a better transmission of place-of-articulation information compared to normally spoken logatomes, while fast speaking rate or soft speaking style yields severely degraded recognition scores (even if the effect of speech level was compensated for). Speech with dialect or accent produces a relative increase of error rates of up to 200 % which is consistently reflected in degradation for the articulatory features voicing, manner and place of articulation.

3. The analysis of consonant scores based on articulatory features (AFs) showed that the place of articulation is the least robust AF for the variabilities analyzed in this study. On the other hand, the recognition of voiced vs. unvoiced sounds was less affected by changes in speaking style, effort and rate.

4. The systematic variation of several variabilities enables a comparison of speech-intrinsic and extrinsic factors: For human listeners, the presence of varied speaking rate, effort or dialect results in a degradation of performance which is equivalent to a 1.5-dB-decrease in SNR for a stationary, speech-shaped masking noise (assuming medium speech intelligibility).

5. The phoneme recognition rate was found to correlate with a simple measure of spectral distance to the masking noise ($r = 0.75$), i.e., the spectral characteristics of the masker play an important role in phoneme recognition, which is in line with earlier studies. We also observed that error rates are significantly related to the properties of those alternative phonemes which are spectrally close. This effect was found to be stronger for vowels ($r = -0.75$) than for consonants ($r = -0.57$).

6. While consonant recognition scores reported here coincide well with data from Grant and Walden (1996), differences of up to 12 dB were found across studies in

terms of the SNR corresponding to 50 % intelligibility (Miller and Nicely, 1955; Sroka and Braida, 2005; Phatak and Allen, 2007). Our findings of correlations between recognition rates and phoneme-noise distance can account for parts of these differences (and hence confirm findings of Phatak and Allen (2007)). However, more factors (such as, e.g., the number of response alternatives, the number of phonemes and coarticulation effects in the presented speech items, and the selection and speaking style of the speaker) obviously contribute to the differences across studies. The Oldenburg Logatome Corpus employed here avoids some of these (unwanted) variability effects by using a fixed word format and providing a number of different speaking styles with the same respective talker. It therefore produces phoneme scores that are in between the extreme high or low scores found in the literature.

2.7 Acknowledgements

Supported by the DFG (SFB/TRR 31 'The active auditory system'; URL: http://www.uni-oldenburg.de/sfbtr31). The OLLO speech database has been developed as part of the EU DIVINES Project IST-2002-002034.

We thank Matthias Wächter and Markus Röhl for conducting several of the listening experiments. We also thank Alfred Mertins, Jörn Anemüller, Kirsten Wagener, Stéphane Dupont, and Christophe Ris for their support and contributions to this work.

3

Effect of speech-intrinsic variations on human and automatic speech phoneme recognition

Abstract

A comparison between automatic speech recognition (ASR) and human speech recognition (HSR) is performed as prerequisite for identifying sources of errors and improving feature extraction in ASR. Experiments are carried out with a logatome database that consists of nonsense syllables. Special focus is laid on the effect of speech-intrinsic variabilities, such as speaking rate and effort, altered pitch, and the presence of dialect and accent. To analyze the information loss caused by feature extraction, ASR features are resynthesized to audible utterances and presented to human listeners. The overall human-machine-gap in terms of the signal-to-noise ratio was found to be 15 dB. A bottom-up contribution of 10 dB to this gap (associated with imperfect feature extraction) was estimated by comparing results with original and resynthesized speech, while 5 dB of the gap were attributed to the classifier (i.e., the top-down component). Intrinsic variabilities severely degrade recognition performance by up to 120 %. An analysis of utterances with different speaking rates showed that phoneme duration is an important cue for discrimination of vowels in HSR, but not in ASR at low SNRs. These results highlight the limitations of ASR as well as the potential of appropriate spectro-temporal features and more appropriate classification algorithms.

3.1 Introduction

Automatic speech recognizers have continuously been improved during the last decades, but no system exists yet that shows the same performance as human listeners. While humans have little difficulties in dealing with recognition in acoustically challenging situations, automatic speech recognition (ASR) lacks the same robustness that is achieved by the auditory system. This observation has inspired several studies that compare the performance of human speech recognition (HSR) and ASR, with the ultimate goal of learning from the biological blueprint to improve automatic recognizers.

The gap between HSR and ASR was shown to widen in noise, or when the complexity of the recognition task increases (Lippmann, 1997). For very complex tasks (such as the transcription of spontaneous speech) the error rates of ASR were reported to be an order of magnitude higher than those of HSR. In more recent studies that compare HSR and ASR, various of aspects of the robustness against extrinsic sources of variation have been covered: The effect of high lexical processing has been studied, and human listeners were found to make better use of lexical, syntactic and semantic information during speech understanding (Shen et al., 2008). Other studies analyzed the effect of low-lexical processing, by comparing HSR and ASR phoneme recognition: Sroka and Braida (2005) investigated the effect of additive noise and high- and lowpass filtered speech. Adding noise resulted in considerable differences between HSR and ASR (with an SNR shift of approx. 10 dB), while high- und lowpass-filtering reduced (and for some conditions even eliminated) the gap. The effect of stationary and time-varying masking noises on phoneme recognition is studied in the framework of the Consonant Challenge, which was proposed in (Cooke and Scharenborg, 2008) and which provides both HSR scores and baseline ASR results. The ASR baseline error rates were found to be 85 % higher for clean speech compared to HSR on the consonant recognition task.

While the robustness of ASR systems against extrinsic variability (e.g., additive or convolutive noise) has been studied extensively and has therefore been understood quite well, the robustness against *intrinsic* variations of speech is far less understood (i.e., the natural variability that is produced by the talker, such as, for example, speaker physiology, accent and dialect, speaking rate, speaking style (e.g. formal vs. spontaneous style), and emotional state). Even though human listeners are remarkably robust in their recognition performance against these intrinsic variations, this does not apply to ASR: The variations were found to degrade the performance of automatic recognizers, even when the acoustic conditions are optimal (Benzeguiba et al., 2007). For example, the overall recognition performance was decreased when the speaking rate is changed; this affected HSR to a lesser extent than ASR (Krause and Braida, 1995; Stern et al., 1996).

The standard approach to ASR is to extract short-time Fourier transform of quasi-stationary speech signals, and use the spectral envelope of these segments as input for the classifier. To assess the relative contribution of non-ideal speech features (that limit the bottom-up-processing in ASR) and non-ideal pattern recognizers (that limit the training- and reference-based top-down processing in ASR), these features may be resynthesized, i.e., the features can be converted to audible signals, which can be presented to human listeners (who serve as 'optimal classifier' in this case). Listening experiments based on resynthesized speech have been conducted earlier: Leonard (1984) performed tests with clean digits that were resynthesized from linear prediction coefficients. The recognition accuracy based on the majority of three listeners was 99.9 %, indicating that signals resynthesized from the spectral envelope of short-time fragments of speech are sufficient in acoustically optimal conditions. Peters et al. (1999) carried out a comparison of HSR and ASR performance with unaltered and resynthesized speech. Feature vectors calculated from noisy digits were converted to audible signals based on an analytical processing scheme. When comparing HSR and ASR with informational equivalent features, the digit error rate of ASR was found to be 13.1 %, while the scores for the original and resynthesized features was 2.9 % and 10.7 %, respectively. However, the effect of a specific masking level as well as speech-intrinsic variability is not investigated in these studies.

A more detailed analysis of the man-machine-gap with respect to robustness against intrinsic speech variability appears to be worthwhile in order to characterize and copy to ASR the assumed invariance operation the human listeners seem to perform with the variants of speech utterances belonging to the same speech symbol. Hence, a detailed man-machine-comparison with special focus on such variations is performed here. The variabilities under consideration were speaking rate, speaking effort (i.e., loudly and softly spoken speech), speaking style (utterances with rising pitch), and dialect and accent. The influence of feature extraction is taken into account by presenting resynthesized speech to human listeners. The resynthesis is based on mel-frequency cepstral coefficients (Davis and Mermelstein, 1980) which are the most common features in ASR. The original signals were also presented in listening tests to evaluate the

HSR-ASR-gap independently of the feature extraction stage, and to quantify the bottom-up and top-down processing in ASR, as shown in Fig. 3.1.

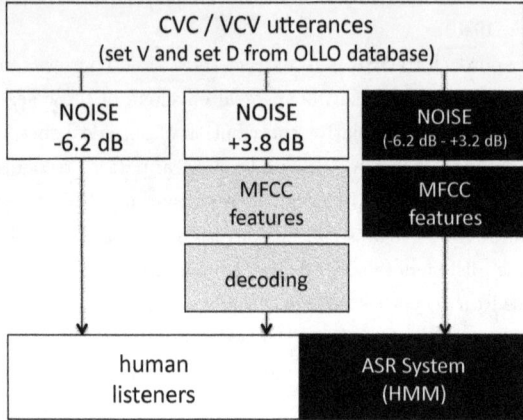

FIG. 3.1 *Overview of different experimental conditions. Original and resynthesized signals were presented to human listeners; the results were compared to the performance of automatic recognizers.*

For similar experimental conditions, the same speech database with nonsense syllables was employed for ASR and HSR tests. Using the same database has the advantage of suppressing unwanted variability that is, e.g., caused by inter-individual differences across speakers. This might be especially important when investigating changes in speaking rate, as different talkers often employ different strategies to produce speech in the desired way (Krause and Braida, 2003). Alternatively, the phoneme recognition may be analyzed with a task that is based on continuous, meaningful speech, which adds the element of imperfect language modelling in ASR (Shen et al., 2008). The focus of this study is however laid on the low-level acoustic-phonetic modeling by using nonsense utterances, which prevents human listeners from exploiting context knowledge.

3.2 Methods

3.2.1 Speech database

The corpus used for this study is the Oldenburg Logatome Corpus (OLLO) (Wesker et al., 2005). It consists of nonsense utterances (logatomes), which are composed according to phonetic and phonotactic rules. The logatomes are combinations of consonant-vowel-consonant (CVC) and vowel-consonant-vowel (VCV) with identical outer phonemes. The database is used to analyze the performance of human listeners in phoneme recognition where the task is to identify the middle phoneme, which limits the number of response alternatives and allows for an easy realization of HSR tests. Since OLLO contains speech material collected from 50 speakers with several repetitions for each logatome, it is also suitable to train and evaluate automatic speech recognizers. The phonemes contained in the database are critical in either human or automatic recognition of speech, so that significant differences in recognition rates may already be obtained with smaller test sets. The phonemes contained in the database as well as other important properties are listed in Table 3.1.

Note that not all possible combinations of VCVs and CVCs have been recorded in order to limit the recording time. Since the recognition task is to identify the middle phoneme of logatomes, all consonant phonemes were recorded for VCVs, and all vowels were used for the CVCs.

Number of speakers	50 (25 male, 25 female)
Number of different VCVs	70 (five outer vowels (/a/, /ɛ/, /ɪ/, /ɔ/, /ʊ/) combined with 14 central consonants (/b/, /d/, /f/, /g/, /k/, /l/, /m/, /n/, /p/, /s/, /ʃ/, /t/, /v/, /ts/))
Number of different CVCs	80 (eight outer consonants (/b/, /d/, /f/, /g/, /k/, /p/, /s/, /t/) combined with 10 central vowels (/a/, /ɛ/, /ɪ/, /ɔ/, /ʊ/, /aː/, /e/, /i/, /o/, /u/))
Number of different logatomes	150
Number of speaking styles	5 + reference condition 'normal' (fast, slow, loud, soft, question)
Number of dialects/accents	4 + reference condition 'no dialect' (East Frisian, Bavarian, East Phalian, French)
Utterances per speaker	2,700 (150 logatomes x 3 repetitions x 6 speaking styles)
Total number of logatomes	133,403
Utterances labeled as containing unwanted sounds	1,820
Number of utterances per dialect/accent	~2,700
Number of utterances per variability	~27,000
Number of utterances per central consonant	~4,450
Number of utterances per central vowel	~7,100

TABLE 3.1 *Properties of the OLLO speech database.*

Variabilities and speakers

The choice of variabilities was based on ASR experiments with annotated test corpora that compared the performance of automatic recognizers with these variabilities present or not. The variabilities under consideration included speaker's gender, age and dialect, speaking style/effort (which also relates to pitch), rate of speech, and breathing noise. The largest impact on performance was observed for the variabilities speaking rate (fast vs. slow), speaking style (affirmation vs. question), speaking effort (loud vs. soft), and dialect/accent. The latter was integrated in the database by including logatomes of dialect speakers from different regions of Germany and from the French-speaking part of Belgium. Ten speakers originating from the northern part of Germany (Oldenburg near Bremen and Hannover) were recorded. The spoken language in this region is usually considered as standard German (Kohler, 1995). We will refer to this category as 'no dialect' (ND). Subjects with dialect originated from the Northern part of Germany (East Frisian dialect, EF), from East Phalia (EP) near Magdeburg, and from Bavarian places near Munich (BV). The French-speaking participants were recorded in Mons (Belgium). Five female and five male speakers from each region were recorded, resulting in a total of 50 speakers. The age of subjects varied between 18 and 65 years. Each logatome was recorded in 'neutral/clear' speaking style as a reference. In addition, one of the five selected variabilities (i.e., fast and slow speaking rate, loud and soft speaking style, and condition 'question' which refers to rising pitch) was altered for each of the subsequent recordings. To provide a broad test and training basis for ASR experiments and to enable an analysis of intra-individual differences, each logatome was recorded three times which resulted in $150 \times (5+1) \times 3 = 2,700$ logatomes per speaker. Additionally, for German speakers 72 German words which are part of the monosyllabic rhyme test (Kollmeier and Wallenberg, 1989) and 20 German sentences part of the Goettingen sentence test (Kollmeier et al., 1997) were included. Participants from Belgium recorded 20 French sentences. This speech material is phonetically balanced and can be used for ASR speaker adaptation.

Recording conditions and postprocessing

Speakers were asked to read the transcription of a logatome and speak it in one of the six variabilities. They were supervised during the recordings and periodically reminded to speak in the desired manner. All VCV stimuli were produced with front stress. During postprocessing, the silence before and after each logatome was limited to 500 ms. Signals were then normalized to 99 % amplitude and stored with 16 bit resolution. They were low-pass filtered with 8 kHz cutoff frequency and sampled down to 16 kHz. Details of the recording conditions are documented in (Meyer et al., 2009). The OLLO corpus was phonetically time-labeled, i.e., temporal positions of phoneme boundaries have been determined for each utterance, making it suitable for tasks such as training of phoneme recognizers using an enhanced version of forced alignment performed with a hidden Markov model. All 150 logatomes were transcribed in the

SAM phonetic alphabet (SAMPA) and the transcription was used as input for the time-labeling procedure.

Availability of speech material and test results

The OLLO database, including a detailed description, wordlists, labeling files, technical specifications and calibration data (normalization coefficients and dB (SPL) values) is freely available for research in HSR and ASR. The uncompressed corpus is approx. 6.4 GB in size and contains a total of approximately 140,000 files corresponding to 60 hours of speech. It can be downloaded from http://medi.uni-oldenburg.de/ollo.

3.2.2 Preparation of speech stimuli

Speech intelligibility tests with human listeners included two conditions, i.e. the presentation of noisy (but otherwise unaltered) signals and listening tests with speech tokens that were resynthesized from ASR features, i.e., feature vectors used internally by the speech recognizer are decoded to acoustic speech signals.

Unaltered speech signals from the OLLO database are used to measure the overall gap between human and automatic recognizers in the presence of intrinsic variabilities and additive noise. Speech-shaped noise is added to the signals to prevent ceiling effects (cf. Section 3.2.4). A second experimental condition covers the aspect of resynthesized speech. The resynthesis of speech is based on the most common features in ASR, i.e., mel-frequency cepstral coefficients (MFCCs). Since the calculation of MFCCs results in a loss of information, these signals sound unnatural (like synthesized speech). For example, the speaker's identity or even gender are usually not recognizable. Nevertheless, resynthesized speech items remain intelligible in the absence of noise (Demuynck et al., 2004). To allow for a valid comparison, the presented recognition scores were obtained with noisy speech. By adding noise, redundant information in the speech signal is masked, so that intelligibility is potentially decreased. The reduction of redundancy might be particularly critical in the presence of speech-intrinsic variabilities.

Calculation of cepstral coefficients

MFCCs are a compact representation of speech signals and have been successfully applied to the problem of ASR (Davis and Mermelstein, 1980). This compact representation has been optimized to retain the information necessary for automatic speech recognition, while information about speech quality and the invidual speaker is mostly discarded. Specifically, the phase information and fine structure of the spectrum are disregarded. However, this may be detrimental in noisy conditions, because some of the information exploited by humans for speech perception in noise is removed. For example, using the phase information in ASR has been found to be beneficial (Schlueter and Ney, 2001).

In order to calculate MFCC features from speech, signals with 16 kHz sampling frequency are windowed with 30 ms Hanning windows and a frame shift of 10 ms. Each frame undergoes the same processing steps: Calculation of the amplitude spectrum, reduction of the frequency resolution using a mel-scaled filterbank and calculating the logarithm and the inverse discrete cosine transformation (IDCT) of its output. Twelve of the lower coefficients plus an additional energy feature are selected for the ASR experiments and HSR tests with resynthesized speech.

This results in (mostly decorrelated) cepstral coefficients, where lower coefficients characterize the coarse structure of the spectrum, while higher coefficients code the fine structure caused by the excitation of the vocal tract. In standard ASR systems as employed in this work, the latter are usually disregarded. In the presented experiments, a frame shift of 12.5 ms with half-overlapping windows was chosen. Input signals had a sampling frequency of 16 kHz; the application of the Mel-filterbank and the IDCT results in twelve cepstral coefficients. These feature vectors were used for the ASR tests as well as the basis for resynthesized speech presented to human listeners.

Resynthesis of cepstral coefficients

In order to reconstruct an acoustic speech signal from MFCC features, the spectral envelope has to be reconstructed from the feature data. This is done using a linear neural network that inverts the discrete cosine transformation. In this study, training material from the OLLO training subset has been used to determine the optimal weights of the neural net. In a second step, the spectral fine structure and phase information has to be estimated. Since the listeners' knowledge should be limited to the information contained in the features, additional information such as voicing or fundamental frequency should not be added during the decoding process, i.e., an artificial excitation signal has to be used. This signal may be either a pulse train (which corresponds to voiced excitation of the vocal tract), a noise signal (as for voiceless excitation) or a superposition of these. The artificial excitation signal is defined by the fundamental frequency and the amount of voicing. For high-quality resynthesis, these parameters need to be extracted from the speech signal. In this study however, it would give human listeners an unfair advantage against the ASR system and is therefore not used.

The excitation signal $p(t)$ is combined with the smoothed magnitude spectrogram $|E(kT, \omega)|$ by calculating the dot product of $|E(kT, \omega)|$ and the magnitude spectrogram of $p(t)$ (i.e., $|P(kT, \omega)|$, where k is the frame index, T is the frame shift and ω is the frequency tab). This leads to the target magnitude spectrogram $|Y(kT, \omega)|$ of the resynthesized signal. In order to construct the phase information, an algorithm proposed in (Griffin and Lim, 1984) is used. This algorithm iteratively decreases the squared error between $|Y(kT, \omega)|$ and the magnitude spectrogram $|X_i(kt, \omega)|$ of the resynthesized signal. At each iteration i, the next estimate of the time signal $x_{i+1}(t)$ is constructed from the target magnitude spectrum $|Y(kT, \omega)|$ combined with the phase spectrum of the previous estimate of the time signal $x_i(t)$. The algorithm usually converges in less than 100 iterations, even if white noise is used as initial time signal $x_1(t)$ (Griffin and Lim, 1984; Demuynck et al., 2004).

Since the properties of the excitation signal is crucial parameter for the overall quality of resynthesis, preliminary tests were performed which showed that - in the presence of speech-shaped noise - intelligibility is higher when a pulse train is used as excitation signal (instead of noise or a mixed noise-pulse signal), which is therefore used for all presented HSR tests with resynthesized speech. A fundamental frequency of 130 Hz was chosen for all presentations. Due to the fixed fundamental frequency, resynthesized speech sounds artificial and tinny, but remains understandable in the absence of noise. This algorithm was kindly supplied by the Katholieke Universiteit Leuven.

HSR scores are usually very close to 100 % for the clean condition, both for the unaltered signals and the signals derived from cepstral coefficients. In (Meyer et al., 2006), the lowest recognition rate observed for non-dialect speech was 99.1 % for a similar task. This clearly demonstrates the excellence of the human auditory system, but does not allow for a valid analysis of phoneme confusions, because differences at very low or high error rates often are outside the range of reliably observable differences. Hence, a continuous masking noise with a frequency characteristic of normal speech (Dreschler et al., 2001) is used to increase the difficulty of the listening task. In case of resynthesized speech, noise is added before MFCCs are calculated from the original signals.

Pilot measurements with one test subject showed that a ceiling effect is always observed when the same SNR is used for resynthesized and original signals, i.e. the recognition rates are either too low for the first or too high for the second condition to obtain valid and comparable results in reasonable measurement time. Based on these first measurements, the SNR for each condition was chosen to produce approximately the same recognition rates. Resynthesized and original signals were presented at an SNR of 3.8 dB and -6.2 dB, respectively.

The training of the neural net used for decoding was also carried out with noisy MFCC features. For the HSR experiments, resynthesized and unaltered signals are subject of measurements. At the same time, the SNR had to be varied, which aggravates a direct comparison because two parameters were changed at the same time. The change of SNR was necessary in order to ensure significant results, as recognition rates are close to chance performance for resynthesized signals at -6.2 dB SNR and > 90 % for original signals at an SNR of 3.8 dB. Preliminary experiments showed that HSR scores for the two test conditions are similar if the SNR is -6.2 dB for the unprocessed signals and 3.8 dB for the resynthesized signals, respectively.

3.2.3 HSR and ASR test and training sets

Two sets of logatomes, which are subsets of the OLLO corpus, were defined to analyze the effects of speech-intrinsic variabilities. From the 50 speakers in the database, those speakers were chosen as being representative for the corpus that produced recognition rates for a standard ASR task which were closest to the average recognition rate: MFCC features with delta and accelaration coefficients were used as input for a HMM, with the same configuration as described in Section 3.2.4. The HMM was trained with utterances from 49 speakers and was subsequently tested with logatomes from the remaining speaker. This procedure was performed for all speakers in the corpus, and

	Set V	Set D
Speakers	S01M, S02F, S06M, S08F	S01M, S02F, S17M, S19F, S23F, S30M, S32M, S40F, S41F, S42M
Dialect / accent	No dialect	No dialect, East Frisian, Bavarian, East Phalian, French
Speaking styles	Normal, fast, slow, soft, loud, question	Normal
HSR		
Stimuli	Orig. signals (-6.2 dB SNR), Resynth. signals (3.8 dB SNR)	Orig. signals (-6.2 dB SNR), Resynth. signals (3.8 dB SNR)
No. of utterances per listener	3,600	1,500
No. of listeners	6	5
No. of presentations	2 × 21,600	2 × 7,500
ASR		
No. of test utterances	10,749	4,481
No. of training utterances	16,159	17,797

TABLE 3.2 *Subsets of the OLLO database used HSR and ASR experiments. The sets are used to analyze the influence of variabilities such as speaking rate and effort (Set V) or dialect (Set D). The supplements 'M' and 'F' denote the gender of the respective talker.*

the results were used to compile subsets that yield similar overall performance as the complete set of talkers.

Set V aims at differences caused by speaking rate, effort, and style. It contains data from four speakers without regional dialect (ND = no dialect) with six variabilities. Set D contains utterances from two speakers from each dialect/accent region with normal speaking style. The properties of these sets are listed in Table 3.2.

For measurements with Set D, the SNR was calculated by relating the root-mean-square (rms) value of the speech segments of each audio signal and the rms value of a masking noise of equal length. A simple voice detection algorithm based on an energy criterion was used to extract connected speech segments. Random control samples were chosen to control proper functioning of that algorithm. For utterances from Set V, a different SNR calculation scheme was applied: In this case, the rms levels of the whole utterance (including silence) and a noise segment of equal length were used to adjust the SNR. Since the length of silence before and after each logatome is 500 ms and because the variation of temporal spread of identical logatomes is relatively small, this corresponds to a fixed offset which was found to be 3.8 dB compared to the SNR calculation scheme mentioned above. For clarity, the SNR values for Set V are converted to the first mentioned method.

The ASR test sets contained the same utterances which were also used in HSR experiments. The two additional repetitions recorded for OLLO which are not contained in the HSR test set were also included. This violates the rule of having exactly equal conditions for HSR and ASR, but increases the amount of test data by a factor of three at the same time. Since speakers were recorded in one session, the differences between utterances are expected to be negligible. Moreover, from the three recordings of each logatome in each variability an arbitrary file has been chosen for HSR test, which prevents a systematic error when using three recordings instead of one. The extension of the test data is an important argument regarding statistics: Five human listeners participated in HSR experiments, while only one ASR recognition engine was used which reduces the test data compared to HSR. When it comes to comparing differences between phoneme recognition scores, the increased number of utterances outweighs the differences of the test sets because of reasons of statistical relevance.

ASR training was carried out with utterances from speakers not included in the test set, resulting in speaker-independent recognizers. For tests with Set V, speech files from six speakers without dialect (but with varying speaking effort and rate) where used for training. For Set D, speech files from 40 speakers with all dialects were chosen for the training process. The phonemes, gender and the systematically varied parameters were equally distributed in the training and test set. ASR recognition scores were obtained for different SNRs, using the same masking noise as for the HSR measurements, as described above. The same SNR was used for training and test, resulting in a matched training-test-condition.

3.2.4 Experimental setup

Tests with human listeners

Six normal-hearing listeners (three male, three female) without noticeable regional dialect participated in the listening tests for Set V; five of these subjects (two male, three female) also participated in tests with Set D. The listeners' hearing loss did not exceed 15 dB at more than one frequency and +10 dB at more than two frequencies in the pure tone audiogram. Signals were presented in a soundproof booth via audiological headphones (Sennheiser HDA200). An online freefield equalization and randomization of logatomes was performed by the measurement software MessOL. Feedback or the possibility to replay the logatome was not given during the test procedure. In order to avoid errors due to inattentiveness, listeners were encouraged to take regular breaks. After a training phase, subjects were presented a sequence of logatomes at a level of 70 dB SPL, i.e., the effect of speech level which is expected to influence recognition of, e.g., softly and loudly spoken utterances, was compensated for. For each presentation, the logatome had to be selected from a list of CVCs or VCVs with the same outer phoneme and different middle phonemes. A touch screen and a computer mouse were used as input devices. In order to avoid speaker adaptation, all resynthesized signals were presented before the subjects listened to the unprocessed speech files. The HSR measurements include 3,600 (Set V) and 1,500 (Set D) presentations per listener and test condition (i.e. the presentation of original and resynthesized signals). The cumulative measurement time was approximately 130 hours, including pauses and instructions for listeners. It was distributed across different days (including a daily training session prior to data recording) in order not to exceed three hours of measurement for each day and each subject.

Automatic speech recognition test setup

ASR experiments were carried out with a Hidden Markov Model (HMM) with three states and eight Gaussian mixtures per HMM state. The system was set up to resemble the closed test which was used for human intelligibility tests, i.e. confusions could only occur for the middle phonemes. This was achieved by grouping utterances with the same outer phonemes, and subsequently using each group to train and test the back-end.

The same MFCC features have been used for the ASR test as for the resynthesized signals in HSR experiments. Additional delta and acceleration features were added to the 13 cepstral coefficients, yielding a 39-dimensional feature vector per time step. Without these features, ASR performance would drop dramatically, because the HMM is not capable of modeling all dynamic aspects of speech as well as humans can. Delta features are calculated directly from cepstral features, i.e. no further information is extracted from the speech signal, so that the principle of supplying ASR and HSR with the same amount of information is not violated.

3.2.5 Outcome measures

Articulatory features and transmitted information

The phoneme confusions are analyzed based on the transmitted information of articulatory features (AFs) as proposed in (Miller and Nicely, 1955). The AFs under consideration and their respective feature values are presented in Table 3.3. For each AF, a confusion matrix is derived from the phoneme confusion matrix by grouping the matrix elements that correspond to the recognition or misclassification of a certain feature value (e.g., all elements that correspond to presentation of an unvoiced sound, when a voiced sound was classified). The transmitted information (or mutual information) is a measure of how well each of these features was recognized.

It is given by $T(x, y) = -\sum_{i,j} p_{ij} \log \frac{p_i p_j}{p_{ij}}$, with p_i and p_j denoting the *a-priori* and *a-posteriori* probabilities for the stimuli, and p_{ij} denoting a matrix element of the confusion matrix. The relative transmitted information is given by $T_r(x, y) = T(x, y)/H(x)$ with the source entropy $H(x) = \sum_i p_i \log(p_i)$. The transmission scores derived directly from the confusion matrices for consonants and vowels serve as measure for consonant and vowel recognition.

Phoneme duration

In order to analyze the dependency of phoneme duration and recognition for the presented experiments, the distribution of the duration of each middle phoneme was determined. The duration was derived from phoneme boundaries that were automatically estimated using a modified forced alignment algorithm, i.e., a trained automatic recognizer was used to find the optimal alignment between the (given) phoneme string and the utterance (cf. Section 3.2.1). In contrast to standard forced alignment, the algorithm employed can account for pronunciation variants (Kipp et al., 1996), which is an important feature for logatomes spoken by speakers with dialect or accent. For each of the ten bins in the duration histogram, the recognition rate for the items was calculated and compared to the according duration. To obtain statistically

Articulatory feature	Feature values	Corresponding phonemes
Place	Bilabial	/p/, /b/, /m/
	Alveolar	/f/, /v/
	Labiodental	/t/, /d/, /n/, /s/, /ts/, /l/
	Palato-Alveolar	/ʃ/
	Velar	/k/, /g/
Manner	Plosive	/p/, /t/, /k/, /b/, /d/, /g/
	Nasal	/n/, /m/
	Fricative	/s/, /f/, /v/, /ʃ/, /ts/
	Lat. Approx.	/l/
Voicing	Voiced	/b/, /d/, /g/, /v/, /n/, /m/, /l/
	Unvoiced	/p/, /t/, /k/, /s/, /f/, /ʃ/, /ts/
Backness	Back	/ɔ/, /ʊ/, /o/, /u/
	Front	/a/, /ɛ/, /ɪ/, /aː/, /e/, /i/
Height	Closed	/ɪ/, /ʊ/, /i/, /u/
	Close-mid	/e/, /o/
	Open-mid	/ɛ/, /ɔ/
	Open	/a/, /aː/

TABLE 3.3 *Articulatory features, their feature values, and the phonemes that correspond to a specific feature value (based on the International Phonetic Alphabet proposed by the International Phonetic Association)*

valid results, only bins with more than 50 items were considered for the analysis. Since the ASR test set contained only halve the number of items (with two additional test items compared to the HSR set, but only one ASR systems instead of six listeners) this threshold was set to 25 for ASR.

3.3 Results

3.3.1 Overall performance

Overall HSR and ASR phoneme recognition scores obtained with Sets V and D are presented in Table 3.4. ASR experiments were carried out at various SNRs, while the tests with human listeners were limited to a specific masking level. When conditions with the same SNR are compared, strong differences between HSR with the original signals and ASR are observed. At -6.2 dB SNR, the relative error of ASR is increased by 168 % compared to HSR. The largest differences occur for logatomes spoken with rising pitch ('question') and East Frisian dialect, with absolute differences of over 45 %. The smallest differences were found for speech with a French accent and high speaking rate (with absolute differences of 33.4 % and 36.8 %, respectively).

A similar average HSR performance with Set V is obtained for the original and resynthesized signals (74.5 % and 72.4 % recognition rate, respectively). The information loss induced by the feature calculation and resynthesis can therefore be approximated and amounts to 10 dB (i.e., the SNR difference for original and resynthesized signals). A similar overall ASR performance is obtained at 8.8 dB. The overall gap for this phoneme recognition task to HSR performance is roughly 15 dB, and the gap between HSR performance with resynthesized signals and ASR is 5 dB. Results obtained with Set D are consistent with these observations since the average HSR recognition scores differ by only 0.2 % absolute. At an SNR of 6.8 dB, the ASR performance lies between these scores, indicating that the overall gap in terms of SNR amounts to 13 dB. As before, the gap between this ASR score and the scores from the HSR resynthesis experiments (3 dB) is much smaller than the gap that is related to the front-end.

Intrinsic variations consistently degrade HSR performance compared to the reference condition, with only a few exceptions to this rule ('slow' speaking style and East Frisian dialect for resynthesized signals, 'loud' speaking style for original signals, and high speaking rate for ASR scores at the highest masker level).

The relative increase of errors in the presence of intrinsic variabilities for both HSR conditions and selected ASR experiments is displayed in Fig. 3.2. Scores are presented for ASR experiments for which the same SNR as for the HSR measurements was used (-6.2 and 3.8 dB) and for normally spoken logatomes that resulted in comparable ASR performance (SNR +8.8dB). For HSR, the respective error rate for normal utterances has been used as reference for the relative increase. The ASR reference is the error rate for normally spoken utterances at a SNR of 8.8 dB.

	Average	Normal	Fast	Slow	Loud	Soft	Question
HSR							
Resynth. (3.8 dB)	72.4	76.3	68.0	77.7	68.8	68.5	75.3
Original (-6.2 dB)	74.5	78.6	72.3	77.2	79.3	63.3	76.3
ASR							
clean	80.4	85.3	78.8	82.3	76.6	79.1	80.5
18.8 dB	77.5	83.5	76.1	81.3	73.1	75.9	75.3
13.8 dB	76.0	82.3	72.9	80.7	71.3	73.1	75.6
8.8 dB	72.8	80.4	67.9	78.4	67.0	69.5	73.8
6.8 dB	69.7	76.3	64.5	75.8	65.2	65.8	70.6
3.8 dB	64.5	71.5	60.0	69.5	60.3	59.2	66.2
-1.2 dB	54.0	60.3	50.5	58.4	54.4	47.0	53.6
-6.2 dB	31.8	35.2	35.5	32.2	36.2	21.0	30.5

	Average	No dialect	East Frisian	Bavarian	East Phalian	French
HSR						
Resynth. (3.8 dB)	73.8	77.5	79.2	75.1	71.3	65.7
Original (-6.2 dB)	74.0	81.5	80.9	77.6	70.2	59.7
ASR						
clean	82.1	88.4	84.5	79.1	84.1	74.2
13.8 dB	79.3	87.0	82.5	75.4	78.5	73.2
6.8 dB	73.6	81.5	76.9	71.5	72.4	65.9
3.8 dB	68.5	75.4	72.4	66.8	68.0	59.8
-6.2 dB	34.0	42.6	34.0	36.2	30.8	26.3

TABLE 3.4 *HSR and ASR phoneme recognition scores in %, depending on speech intrinsic variabilities and the SNR. Scores for varied speaking effort, rate and style were obtained with Set V; the results for dialects and accents are based on measurements with Set D (cf. Table 3.2).*

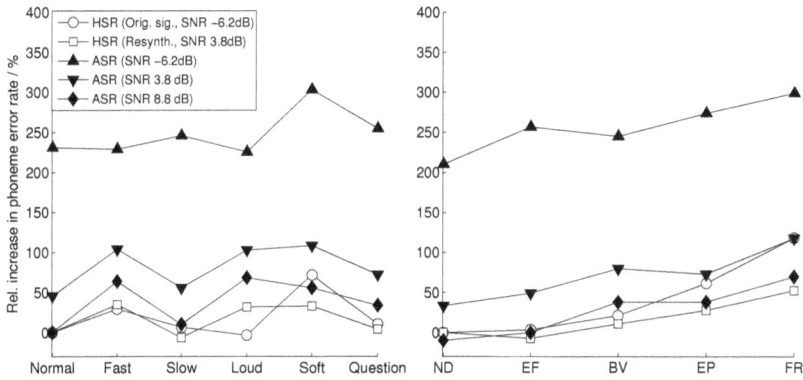

FIG. 3.2 *Relative increase of phoneme error rates for HSR and ASR. The increase is related to the error rate obtained with normally spoken utterances for HSR. All ASR scores are related to normally spoken utterances with a training/test SNR of +8.8 dB (which produced similar performance compared to HSR).*

	Intrinsic variation	Speaker	Listener
HSR			
Original (SNR -6.2 dB)	28.4**	33.1**	7**
Resynth (SNR 3.8 dB)	9.2**	67.7**	7.7**
ASR			
-6.2 dB	50.8**	24.7*	-
-1.2 dB	35.4*	40.9**	-
3.8 dB	28.8*	46.9**	-
8.8 dB	32.9**	48.8**	-
13.8 dB	27.3*	50.3**	-

TABLE 3.5 *Results of an ANOVA of recognition scores: The values denote the proportion of variance explained by the intrinsic variation, speaker's and listener's identity. The asterisks specify the level of significance (* < 5 %, ** < 1 %).*

A comparison of resynthesized and original signals shows that large differences occur for loud and soft speaking style while all other conditions appear to be similarly influenced. The results for the ASR conditions with medium scores (SNR of 3.8 and 8.8 dB) are consistent, i.e., the highest degradations are observed for the conditions 'fast', 'loud, and 'soft'. At high masking levels, ASR produces 200 % higher error rates than the ASR reference condition. The conditions 'soft' and 'question' yield a further degradation, while the other conditions do not. In the presence of dialect and accent, the errors of both HSR conditions increase (in the order East Frisian, Bavarian, East Phalian, and French). When listening to the original, dialected speech, the human error rates are up to 120 % higher compared to the reference condition. For ASR, similar results were obtained, with the exception that Bavarian results in slightly increased errors compared to East Phalian.

An analysis of variance was performed to test the significance of several parameters that may influence the recognition scores obtained with original signals and Set V: Table 3.5 shows the percentage of variance explained by the variables 'intrinsic variation' (speaking rate, effort, and style), and choice of speaker and listener (the latter only for HSR experiments). The results show that the variabilities from Set V have a significant impact on the overall recognition performance in HSR and ASR. There are however shifts in the importance between the parameters 'variability' and 'speaker', which are discussed in the next section.

3.3.2 Information transmission

The confusion matrices for consonants, vowels and several articulatory features were used to calculate the relative transmitted information T_r associated with these features, as described in Section 3.2.5. Fig. 3.3 presents the scores in dependency of speaking style, rate and effort, and dialect and accent for both HSR and selected ASR conditions. The analysis based on AFs shows that conditions with similar average performance (both HSR conditions and ASR at +8.8dB SNR) exhibit considerable variations, both among different AFs and intrinsic variations. Scores obtained with resynthesized signals are in most cases higher than scores for original logatomes for consonant and consonant-associated features (left and center panels in Fig. 3.3). For vowel associated features (right panels), the opposite result is found. High speaking effort ('loud') yields above-average performance for original signals, which can mainly be attributed to the voicing and place feature. This is however not observed for resynthesized features, for which only medium transmission scores are obtained.

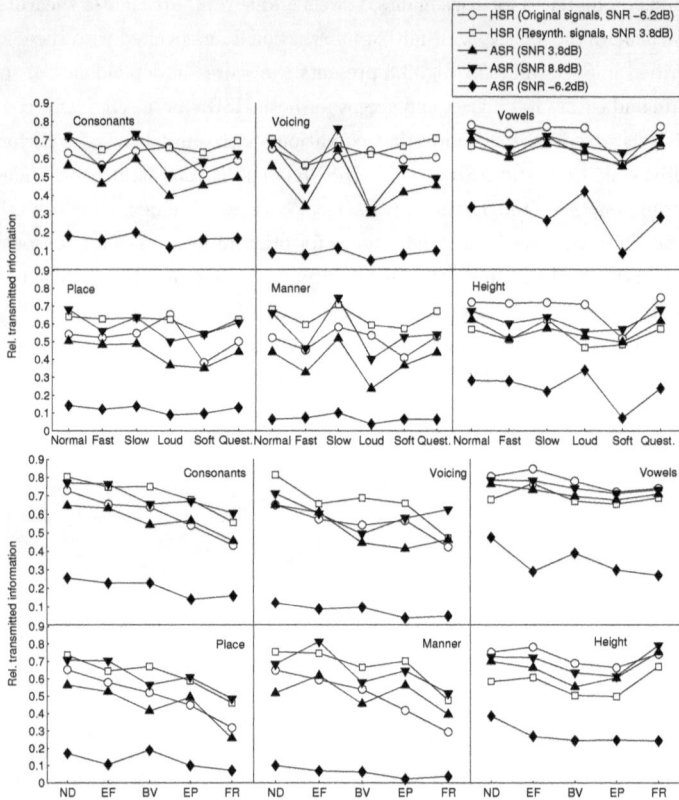

FIG. 3.3 *Information transmission scores for consonants and consonant-associated features (left and middle panels) and for vowels and the articulatory feature 'height' (right panels), depending of speech-intrinsic variations which are contained in Set V (upper plots) and Set D (lower plots; ND = 'no dialect', EF = 'East Frisian', BV = 'Bavarian', EP = 'East Phalian', FR = 'French')). The categorical variabilities are depicted as connected line graphs for reasons of readability.*

The overall low performance for original signals and low speaking effort ('soft') is reflected in the T_r-scores for all articulatory features, with the exception of voicing. For ASR, a strong dependence of the variability is observed for voicing: While normally and slowly spoken logatomes result in relatively high values for this feature, it is strongly degraded for the categories 'fast' and 'loud' (with degradations of 36 % and 53 % compared to the reference condition 'normal').

3.3.3 Phoneme duration

The distributions of phoneme duration for utterances with high and low speaking rate, as well as for normally spoken utterances are shown in Fig. 3.4. The durations were derived from the output of the forced alignment procedure, as described in Section 3.2.5. The categories 'loud' and 'soft' did not significantly change phoneme duration compared to the reference condition and are therefore not shown in the plot. As expected, fast and slow speaking style differ in phoneme duration from normal speaking style. This is reflected both in the average durations and the 5 % / 95 % quantiles for variabilities fast (with 103 ms duration in average and 40/200 ms for the quantiles), slow (avg.: 255 ms, quantiles: 70/550 ms) and normal (avg.: 146 ms, quantiles: 45/316 ms). However, the distributions of durations for different speaking styles exhibit a considerable overlap. An analysis of variance was carried out for the phoneme duration with the explanatory parameters speaker, phoneme index and speaking style. All of these parameters were found to significantly contribute to the observed variance ($p < 0.01$). The speaking style had the largest impact on the variance of duration, followed by phoneme index and the choice of speaker. When considering a single speaker and a single phoneme, the effect of changes in speaking rate is much more noticeable, as the distributions almost show no overlap in many cases. An example is shown in the right panel of Fig. 3.4.

Changes in speaking rate were found to affect both HSR and ASR recognition (Table 3.4), especially when the rate was increased. The dependency of duration and recognition rate was analyzed on phoneme level for HSR and ASR scores (Fig. 3.5). Both HSR conditions are shown, as well as the ASR scores for which an identical masking level as in HSR was used (-6.2 dB) and which showed similar overall performance (SNR of 8.8 dB).

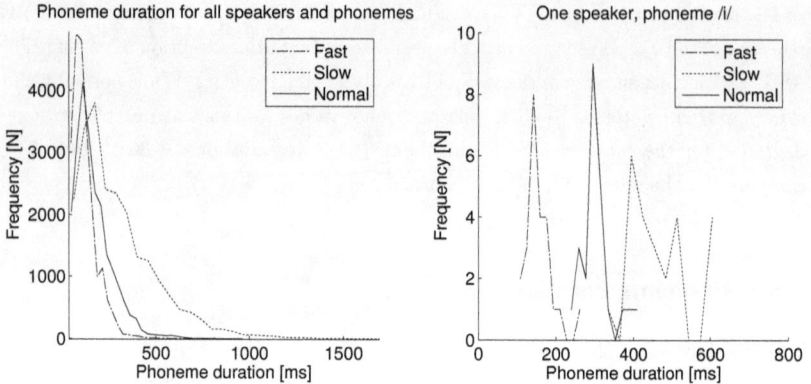

FIG. 3.4 *Distribution of phoneme duration for fast, slow and normal speaking style, averaged over all speakers and phonemes (left panel) and for a single speaker and the phoneme* /i/ *(right panel). The phoneme duration was derived from the forced alignment labels and analyzed with a histogram with 50 bins (left panel) or 10 bins (right panel).*

When human listeners had to recognize noisy, original signals, the recognition rate of the vowel group D1 = /a/, /e/, /i/, /o/, /u/ (open symbols in Fig. 3.5) decreased with increasing duration of that phoneme. On the other hand, the recognition of the vowels (D2 = /aː/, /ɛ/, /ɪ/, /ɔ/, /ʊ/) is improved for increased duration. This general trend can also be found for the resynthesized signals (lower left panel in Fig. 3.5), however, for some examples (/ɛ/, /ɪ/) this result was not observed. The HSR recognition curves for D1 and D2 intersect at a duration of approximately 170 ms which therefore can be considered as an estimate of the category boundary between short and long vowels for our human listeners. We analyzed the confusions of phonemes in HSR with similar duration (ranging from 140 to 200 ms) and found that the following confusions produced the highest error rates (where the first and second phoneme correspond to the presented and chosen item, respectively): (/a/, /aː/), (/ɛ/, /e/), (/e/, /ɪ/), (/ɪ/, /e/), (/i/, /ɪ/), (/ɔ/, /o/), (/o/, /ʊ/), (/ʊ/, /o/), (/u/, /ʊ/). Hence, the phonemes can be pooled in three groups that contain often confused vowels, i.e., V1 = (/a/, /aː/), V2 = (/ɛ/, /e/, /ɪ/, /i/), and V3 = (/ɔ/, /o/, /ʊ/, /u/). The same groups were found for HSR with resynthesized signals, with the exception of (/ɔ/, /aː/) which corresponds to an inter-group confusion with a high error rate. The corresponding vowel confusion

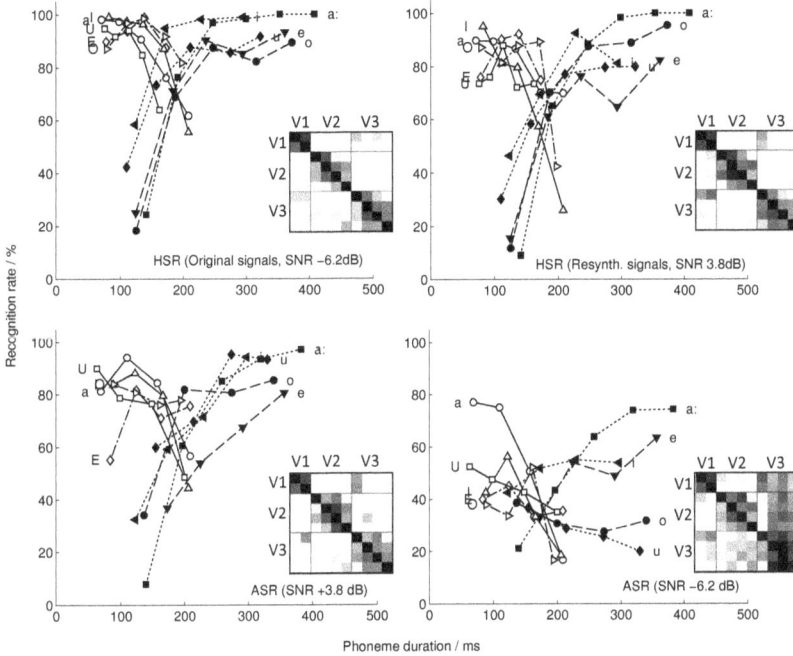

FIG. 3.5 *Relation between phoneme duration and recognition rate for vowel phonemes (two HSR and two ASR conditions). For the phoneme labels in the plot, the SAMPA notation has been used. The inlays show the logarithmic confusion matrix of vowels with durations of 140 to 200 ms. The order of phonemes in each CM is V1 = (/a/, /aː/), V2 = (/ɛ/, /e/, /ɪ/, /i/), V3 = (/ɔ/, /o/, /ʊ/, /u/); the confusion groups are separated by black lines.*

matrices (CMs) are shown as inlays in Fig. 3.5. The same confusion patterns were identified for CMs that included vowels for normal speaking style when all durations were included in the analysis, i.e., the grouping into confusion groups appears not to be affected by the rate of speech.

For ASR at high SNRs, comparable overall trends were found, i.e., phonemes in V1 and V2 were similarly affected by the duration, and errors were mainly restricted to the same confusion groups (with the exception of (/aː/, /ɔ/) which produced high errors for all SNRs in ASR). However, at high masking levels, the dependency between recognition and duration is not as pronounced as in HSR, since a reduced duration does not consistently result in an increased recognition of vowels in D1. For example, the scores for /ɔ/ and /ʊ/ decrease with duration while in the case of other phonemes (/o/ and /e/) a consistent trend is not observed at all. While the highest error rates still correspond to within-group confusions, many confusions occur between (V1, V3) (with an error rate of 33 % compared to 1 % in HSR at the same masking level) and (V2, V3) (with 31 % compared to 0.1 % in HSR). These errors were highly asymmetric, as the confusions (V3, V1) and (V2, V3) exhibited error rates of only 5 %.

In case of consonants (which are not shown in the figure), a strong dependency between duration and recognition was not observed. The fricatives yielded improvements with increasing duration (for ASR more than for HSR, which might result from ceiling effects), while the other consonants showed no consistent trend. The performance increase for fricatives might be due to their relative stationarity in the fricative portion of the consonant, which enables human listeners to perform a temporal integration over a longer time windows, thereby increasing the SNR.

3.4 Discussion

3.4.1 Human vs. machine performance

A direct comparison of human and automatic speech recognition performance shows that average phonemes scores in HSR are superior to the results obtained with standard ASR system. In case of original signals at -6.2dB SNR (Set V), the averaged HSR and ASR accuracies are 74.5 % and 31.8 %, respectively, which corresponds to an increase of word error rate (WER) of 167 %. In order to achieve the same performance, the SNR has to increase by approx. 15 dB for ASR. For dialect measurements, similar results were obtained (HSR: 74.0 %, ASR: 34.0 %, relative increase of WER: 154 %). The gap narrows if the information for human listeners is limited to the information content of MFCCs: The increase of WER between HSR with synthetic stimuli and ASR (both at 3.8 dB SNR) amounts to 29 % (or 5 dB in terms of the SNR, respectively). Again, the results for dialect measurements are consistent with an increase of 20 %.

These results can be compared to HSR and ASR results from other studies: Lippmann (1997) reported an increase of WER by a factor of five for the automatic recognition of alphabet letters (based on classification with a neural net). Cooke and Scharenborg

(2008) used a VCV database to measure ASR performance based on MFCC features with an HMM classifier and found a relative increase of 85 % compared to HSR. In both cases, these results were obtained with clean speech (in contrast to noisy speech employed in this study), which may explain for the differences to the presented experiments. Sroka and Braida (2005) [SB05] analyzed consonant confusions of human and automatic recognizers in speech-weighted noise with VCV utterances. Their results can be compared to SNR-dependent HSR results obtained with the OLLO database (Meyer et al., 2009) [M09] and to the ASR scores from this study (Fig. 3.6). The presented human accuracies from [M09] are based on one speaker from the OLLO database and normally spoken utterances. For comparison, the ASR results for consonant recognition and normal speaking style (based on experiments with Set V) are plotted.

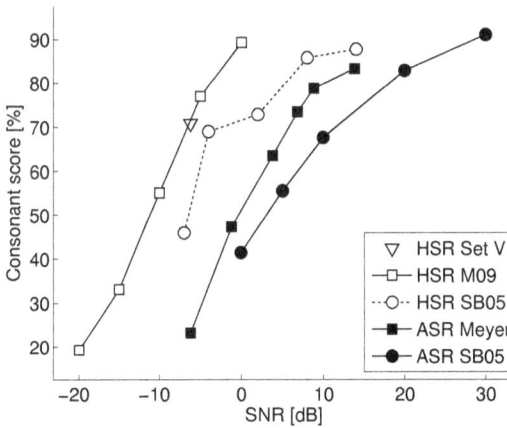

FIG. 3.6 *Comparison of HSR and ASR scores from (Sroka and Braida, 2005) [SB05], (Meyer et al., 2009) [M09], and this study.*

Although the recognition curves exhibit a similar steepness, the results show considerable variations across the experiments: The differences in accuracy are up to 18 % and 13 % absolute for HSR and ASR, respectively. These differences may result from the fact that different speech corpora have been used for the studies, which adds the element of across-speaker variability and differing phoneme inventory. However, the gap between human and machine performance is almost identical for both experiments, and amounts to approximately 12 dB for consonant recognition and normally spoken utterances (SB05: 12.0 dB, M09 and this study: 11.8 dB). This gap was determined by linear interpolation of the recognition curves and calculating the SNR shift that yields the smallest rms error between the HSR and ASR curves. This result is similar to the overall SNR-shift observed in this study: When vowel phonemes are included and scores are averaged over the complete test set, the gap in terms of the SNR is 15 dB (Set V) and 13 dB (Set D).

3.4.2 Effect of resynthesis

The SNRs for HSR tests with original and resynthesized signals were chosen with the aim of producing similar overall performance. The choice of SNRs was based on the presentation of only few test lists to one human listener and proved to be reasonable for other test subjects as well, as the averaged accuracies show a good resemblance: The score differences between resynthesized and original signals for Set V and Set D were 2.1 % and 0.2 %, respectively (cf. Table 3.4). Therefore, the macroscopic information loss caused by MFCCs can be expressed in terms of the signal-to-noise ratio, i.e. the SNR of resynthesized signals has to be 10 dB higher in order to obtain similar recognition performance. Based on this observation, the gap caused by feature calculation (which can be compared to the bottom-up processing in the human auditory system) and by classification (equivalent to the hypotheses-driven top-down processing) can be estimated: With an overall gap of 15 dB and a contribution of 10 dB due to feature calculation and resynthesis, the imperfect back-end in ASR accounts for 5 dB of the SNR shift between human and automatic recognition. This comparatively smaller contribution of the imperfect back-end is consistent with the findings by Jürgens and Brand (2009) who used an auditory model as front-end to ASR and compared the case of perfect a-priori knowledge of the word template to be recognized with the case where only the class of the word template to be recognized was known. While in the first case a near-to-perfect prediction of human recognition scores was possible, in the latter case a gap of approx. 13 dB was observed.

Preliminary measurements have shown that the information contained in MFCCs is sufficient to recognize speech in the absence of noise, since the intelligibility in HSR is not degraded when using resynthesized signals instead of the original ones. This is in line with earlier studies (Leonard, 1984), where a 99.9 % recognition rate was achieved with digits that were resynthesized from features coding the spectral envelope (i.e., linear prediction coefficients). However, the presented measurements in noise clearly show that during the calculation of MFCCs a significant amount of useful information is removed, confirming results from (Peters et al., 1999). The advantage of a judicious choice of SNR in the current study is that this information loss can be quantified in terms of recognition rates and in terms of the SNR.

Apart from the information loss due to feature calculation, other factors might contribute to the degraded speech intelligibility of resynthesized speech: The algorithm that was employed might not optimally reconstruct the time signals, i.e., not all information from the ASR features is perfectly made audible for the listeners. We tried to cover this problem as good as possible by performing pilot experiments with various excitation signals; however, there might still be room for improvement by optimizing, e.g., the pulse form of the excitation signals. Training effects might also play a role in HSR since a fixed fundamental frequency was used for the excitation signal; this resulted in utterances that sounded artificial and unfamiliar to the listeners. Training sessions were performed before each measurement to limit the influence of such training effects.

Original signals exhibit lower consonant transmission scores, which is due to the fact that they were obtained at a lower SNR (-6.2 dB) than the resynthesized signals (+3.8 dB). Vowel phonemes have a higher spectral energy and are therefore less affected by the influence of the additive masker. However, the process of feature calculation and resynthesis appears to influence human vowel recognition stronger than consonant recognition, since vowel-associated features show degraded transmitted information, in spite of the higher SNR (Fig. 3.3). Although MFCCs have been found to encode the spectral shape of vowels well, the reduced frequency resolution may result in inferior differentiation between proximate formants compared to human listeners. The performance drop may also be caused by discarding the phase information which is in accordance with other works where ASR was improved by exploiting phase information (Schlueter and Ney, 2001) or HSR accuracy was reduced by limiting the audible information to the power spectrum (Peters et al., 1999).

3.4.3 Effect of intrinsic variations

Changes in speaking style, rate and effort were found to degrade HSR (with an avg. degradation of 23 %) and ASR (47 % degradation in average at an SNR of 8.8 dB). Instead of considering the effect of variability on the percentage of correct responses, the robustness of HSR and ASR against extrinsic and intrinsic variations may also be expressed in term of the equivalent change in SNR: In HSR, the presence of varied speaking rate, effort or dialect resulted in a degradation of performance which is equivalent to a 1.5-dB-decrease in SNR for a stationary, speech-shaped masking noise (assuming medium speech intelligibility where flooring or ceiling effects are avoided, (Meyer et al., 2009)). These HSR results were obtained with the same test sets (Sets V and D, respectively) that have been employed in the current study. Hence, they can be compared directly to the machine results presented in Table 3.4: In ASR, the effect of intrinsic variations (Set V) has the same effect as an increase of 5 dB of the masking level. This was estimated based on two observations: The ASR accuracy increases almost linearly with approx. 2 % per dB for SNRs from -5 to 15 dB. Second, the average accuracy for normal speech is approximately 10 % higher than speech with changed speaking rate, effort and style.

The results in Table 3.5 show that intrinsic variabilities considerably contribute to the variance of recognition scores in HSR and ASR. The speaker's identity is a second important parameter. It explains at least one third of the variance observed in HSR with original signals and in ASR. Intrinsic variations also have a significant effect on resynthesized speech. In this condition, however, the speaker's *identity* seems to have a more dominant effect than speaking rate, effort and style. This might result from the elimination of speaker-specific, non-redundant cues (e.g., fine phonetic detail) that are removed during feature calculation and resynthesis. The remaining cues may not be sufficient for human listeners to adjust to speaker-specific changes. In case of ASR, the factor 'variability' is more important than in HSR with resynthesized speech, which is consistent with the overall higher sensitivity of ASR against such variations (as described above).

Speech-intrinsic variations also affected the transmitted information associated with several articulatory features (AFs): Compared to human performance, the voicing feature in ASR is degraded by 32 % (averaged over the SNRs shown in Fig. 3.3) when utterances are spoken normally, while manner and place are degraded by 18 and 25 %, respectively. This confirms findings of Sroka and Braida (2005), who observed that the voicing feature was suboptimal recognized by an MFCC-based ASR system when testing phoneme recognition in speech-shaped noise. Cooke and Scharenborg (2008) reported the largest deviations between HSR and ASR for the place feature, while for voicing and manner only small differences were measured. However, these scores were obtained with clean utterances, and can therefore not directly compared to our results.

If resynthesized logatomes contained the same information as the original signals, the scores for resynthesized should be improved compared to the reference condition, since the masking level for resynthesized signals was 10 dB higher than for original utterances (Note that this is a necessary requirement for informationally equivalent signals, not a sufficient requirement). Higher scores for original signals are observed for most of the consonant-associated scores, but the differences are especially small for the voicing feature for the categories 'question', 'slow', and 'soft' and even vanish for the conditions 'loud' and 'fast' (Fig. 3.3). Hence, relevant information employed by human listeners to distinguish voiced and unvoiced consonants is discarded during feature calculation. The information loss also severely degrades the machine performance. This suggests to incorporate at least some aspects of spectral fine structure associated with the recognition of voicing in order to overcome these deficiencies by changing the way in which spectral information is converted into speech cues. The use of such fine-grained cues seems especially important when the speech contains changes in speaking effort and rate. One way to perform such information extraction is the use of Gabor filters (Kleinschmidt, 2003a), for which data-driven algorithms exist that can be employed to estimate suitable filter parameters, and which could be designed to explicetely differentiate between voiced and unvoiced phonemes. This approach is supported by findings from HSR indicating that certain aspects of fine-structure play an important role in word identification and lexical segmentation (Davis et al., 2002). Increased speaking effort ('loud') gave the best consonant recognition for original signals in HSR and is on par with the resynthesized signals (in spite of the differing SNRs), which show no increase for this variability. In ASR, loudly spoken utterances result in the lowest consonant recognition. Similar to the observations for the voicing feature, it seems that human listeners rely on cues contained in speech spoken with increased effort that are lost during feature calculation, which at least partially contributes to the overall low ASR performance for high speaking effort. It is an open question which cues ar the most relevant for this observed large difference between HSR and ASR. Obviously, several AFs are affected (cf. Fig. 3.3), but the perceptual cues associated with these features (especially for the AFs 'place' and 'manner') are not easily accessible. Although the recordings of the OLLO database have been carried out in a quiet environment, the properties of loudly spoken utterances may be similar to the parameters that are changed in Lombard-speech, i.e., speech that has been recorded in noisy surroundings, which results in a slight decrease of consonant duration, changes in spectral properties of fricatives, and maximum burst energy of plosives (Junqua, 1993).

The dependency of vowel duration and recognition rate was presented in Fig. 3.5. In case of HSR and for ASR at high SNRs, two groups of vowel phonemes emerge, for which longer phoneme duration either results in higher recognition performance (D1 = /a/, /e/, /i/, /o/, /u/) or decreased performance (D2 = /aː/, /ɛ/, /ɪ/, /ɔ/, /ʊ/). When spoken at normal speaking rate, vowels from D1 have a longer duration than the phonemes from D2 (Hillenbrand et al., 1995), which was shown to be an important cue for confusion groups in other studies (Phatak and Allen, 2007).

The errors were mainly restricted to confusions within three groups of vowels, (V1 = (/a/, /aː/), V2 = (/ɛ/, /e/, /ɪ/, /i/), V3 = (/ɔ/, /o/, /ʊ/, /u/)), with the exception of the confusion (/ɔ/, /a/). The separation between the groups D1 and D2 was obscured for ASR when the same masking level as in HSR (-6.2 dB SNR) was used; this was attributed to the asymmetric confusions (V1,V2) and (V1,V3). The separation between D1 and D2 observed in HSR suggests that human listeners rely on these temporal cues for vowel recognition in situations in which target phonemes with otherwise similar properties (e.g., formant frequencies) need to be distinguished. Overall vowel recognition with resynthesized signals and in ASR at high SNRs was found to be lower than for original signals; nevertheless, temporal cues also seem to play a major role for differentiation between vowels, while ASR seems not to be able to exploit these cues from noisy features. This results suggest that human listeners employ different strategies to process the information from ASR features compared to a hidden Markov model, e.g. by temporal integration of the signal, or by recognizing the patches of the internal representation belong to the acoustic object that should be recognized. It is unclear if this temporal integration performed by the human auditory system should be considered as a bottom-up detection advantage (due to, e.g., the availability of specialized feature detectors sensitive to signals with a certain duration) or a top-down advantage (due to the availability of "learned" patterns with a certain duration that can serve as a hypothesis for the utterance to be recognized).

One approach to study the bottom-up hypothesis underlying the man-machine gap in this case could be an incorporation of temporal or spectro-temporal information on feature level. Techniques that explicitly cover temporal aspects have been reported to lower error rates in many acoustical scenarios (Hermansky and Sharma, 1999). Gabor filters have been used to extract spectro-temporal information from spectrograms and were found to be very robust again noise since they can be considered matched filters for specific speech features which increases the local SNR (Kleinschmidt, 2002). It remains to be seen if these techniques can help to decrease the degradations in the presence of altered speaking rate.

T_r-scores of resynthesized and original signals were consistent for the dialects under consideration, i.e., both conditions are similarly affected for the majority of the AFs. This suggests that variations caused by the dialects under investigation are equally well encoded by standard ASR features. Overall vowel recognition shows less variation than the recognition of consonants, both for HSR and ASR. For French accent, the height feature is especially well recognized, which is due to reduced number of confusions with closed-mid and open-mid vowels when a closed vowel was presented. The low overall score confirms results from (Garcia Lecumberri et al., 2008), where strong degradations of phoneme accuracy were observed when the first language of talker and listener differed. In this specific case, the degradation is mainly caused by a low recognition of the articulatory features 'place' and 'manner'.

An open question is if the results that were obtained with VCV and CVC utterances are scalable to continuously and conversational speech. Variations in conversational speech are considerable larger then recordings under controlled situations, as speaking rate and effort are subject to frequent changes. However, experiments comparable with our approach would require a database with labeled phonemes and variabilities, which does not yet exist to our knowledge. For the creation of suitable databases, problems such as the ambiguous labeling of phonemes are further aggravated in the presence of strong variations in spoken language, as, e.g., Shriberg et al. (1984) have shown for transcription of children speech.

3.5 Conclusions

- Even for the relatively simple task of phoneme classification, the difference between HSR and ASR remains considerably large: The relative increase of errors is larger than 150 % (assuming medium speech intelligibility). If the information contained in standard ASR features is made audible and presented to human listeners, the gap narrows, but error rates are still 20 % higher for ASR.

- The information loss caused by the calculation and resynthesis of mel-frequency cepstral coefficients can be expressed in terms of the signal-to-noise ratio: Similar recognition results in HSR are obtained when the SNR is 10 dB higher for resynthesized signals instead of unaltered speech files. The overall ASR-HSR gap was found to be approximately 15 dB. It can be decomposed into a bottom-up component (due to imperfect representation of speech by the acoustic features, which amounts to approx. 10 dB in SNR) and a top-down component (caused by imperfect classification techniques, which is about 5 dB in SNR).

- Speech-intrinsic variations were shown to significantly affect both human and machine performance and increased word error rates by up to 120 %. The analysis based on articulatory features showed that for utterances with increased speaking effort and high speaking rate, the differentiation between voiced and unvoiced sounds was especially problematic in ASR. A way to cope with this deficiency may be to modify the scheme of purely spectral features (e.g., by introducing feature components that cover some aspects of spectral fine structure).

- The recognition rates of vowels heavily depend on the speech rate and the duration of these phonemes. Both in HSR and ASR, two groups of vowels were identified that yielded either an improved or a deteriorated *recognition* with increased duration. The highest *error rates* were mainly restricted to specific sets of vowels (V1 = (/a/, /aː/), V2 = (/ɛ/, /e/, /ɪ/, /i/), V3 = (/ɔ/, /o/, /ʊ/, /u/)). While the errors in HSR were consistent over a wide range of signal-to-noise ratios, the ASR confusion patterns were less consistent even at relatively low masking levels. This inability of the ASR system to utilize duration cues in a similar way as in HSR suggests that temporal and spectro-temporal aspects of speech should be incorporated in ASR systems in a more appropriate way, which might be better suited to capture vowel transients.

3.6 Acknowledgments

Supported by the DFG (SFB/TRR 31 'The active auditory system'; URL: http://www.uni-oldenburg.de/sfbtr31). The OLLO speech database has been developed as part of the EU DIVINES Project IST-2002-002034.

We would like to thank Thorsten Wesker, Matthias Wächter, Alfred Mertins, Jörn Anemüller, and Kirsten Wagener for their support and contributions to this work. We also thank Kris Demuynck, who kindly supplied the resynthesis algorithm.

4

Robustness of spectro-temporal features against intrinsic and extrinsic variations in automatic speech recognition

Introduction

The large gap in performance between human speech recognition (HSR) and advanced automatic speech recognition (ASR) is most drastically encountered in adverse acoustic conditions and prohibits ASR technology from being widely used. Consistently, humans outperform machines by at least an order of magnitude (Lippmann, 1997). In recent studies, the gap between human and automatic recognizers was found to be somewhat smaller, but error rates are still more than 150 % higher for ASR than for HSR for a simple phoneme recognition task (Meyer et al., 2007). Human listeners outperform ASR systems not only in acoustically challenging situations (e.g., in the presence of noise or competing talkers), but also when previously unknown clean speech is to be recognized. *Intrinsic* factors such as gender, speaking rate and style, dialect, accent, and vocal effort contribute to the vast variability the human auditory system can cope with much better than current speech recognizers. Hence, finding auditory models that adequately model speech perception has to include the difficult task of modeling human robustness against these intrinsic variations. Our attempt to narrow the gap between human and automatic speech recognition is thus motivated by the idea of transferring auditory processing principles from the human auditory system to ASR.

While many cognitive aspects of speech perception still lie in the dark, there is much progress in the research on signal processing in the more peripheral parts of the auditory system. Findings from a number of physiological experiments in different mammal species showed that a large percentage of neurons in the primary auditory cortex (A1) respond differently to upward- versus downward-moving ripples in the spectrogram of the input. Individual neurons are sensitive to specific spectro-temporal modulation frequencies in the incoming sound signal (Depireux et al., 2001).

The neurophysiological data fit well with psychoacoustic experiments on early auditory features: In (Kaernbach, 2000), a psychophysical reverse correlation technique was applied to masking experiments with semi-periodic white noise. The resulting basic auditory feature patterns are distributed in time and frequency and in some cases consist of several unconnected parts, very much resembling the spectro-temporal receptive field (STRF) of cortical neurons, i.e., the model representation of the excitatory and inhibitory neurons in the auditory cortex.

The STRFs often clearly exceed one critical band in frequency, have multiple peaks and also show tuning to temporal modulation (cf. the example in Fig. 4.1). Still, the STRF patterns are mainly localized in time and frequency, generally spanning at most 250ms and one or two octaves, respectively. In the visual cortex, comparable neural tuning to spatially complex and time-varying patterns is measured with (moving) orientated grating stimuli. The results match very well two-dimensional Gabor functions (De-Valois and De-Valois, 1980). Gabor functions have also been used to approximate auditory STRFs as a sum of time-frequency separable Gabor functions (Qiu et al., 2003). Response patterns derived from STRFs were shown to correlate with articulatory features of phonemes (such as voicing or place or articulation) and result in confusion matrices similar to confusions from human listeners when used as features for ASR (Mesgarani et al., 2007).

The physiological findings have inspired a number of ASR studies that make explicit use of spectro-temporal features instead of relying on the common extraction of purely spectral features and adding delta and double delta derivatives: Kleinschmidt *et al.* used Gabor functions as a simple model for STRFs to compute features for automatic speech recognizers (Kleinschmidt, 2002; Kleinschmidt and Gelbart, 2002; Kleinschmidt, 2003b). The parameters for the Gabor filters (such as spectral and temporal extent and

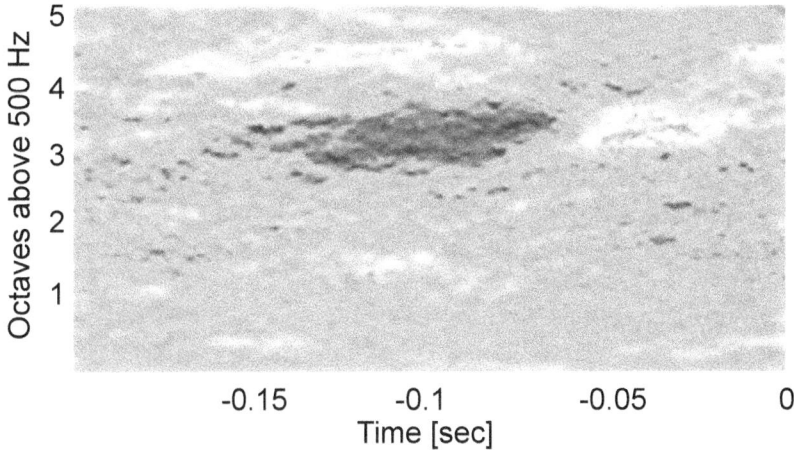

FIG. 4.1 *Spectro-temporal receptive field of a neuron in the primary auditory cortex of the Mongolian gerbil (adapted from Happel et al. (2008)). Dark and light areas denote excitatory and inhibitory regions, respectively.*

modulation frequencies) were optimized in a stochastic process with physiologically motivated constraints. Features obtained from these filters improved digit recognition scores compared to an MFCC baseline by 56 % on average. This approach of spectro-temporal processing by using localized sinusoids matches the neurobiological data and also incorporates other features as special cases: purely spectral Gabor functions perform an analysis similar to Mel-frequency cepstral coefficients (MFCCs) - modulo the windowing function - and purely temporal ones can resemble TRAPS or the RASTA impulse response and its derivatives (Hermansky, 1998) in terms of temporal extent and filter shape.

In a related study, a large number of Gabor features was used to cover a wider range of modulation frequencies, which were subsequently processed with multiple non-linear neural networks to merge the spectro-temporal features streams (Zhao and Morgan, 2008). Heckmann et al. (2008) proposed hierarchical spectro-temporal features based on Gabor filtering for ASR. Similar to the work by Kleinschmidt et al., they used a statistical process to select filter parameters that yield optimal recognition performance.

Gabor filters were applied to the output of a Gammatone filterbank, which resulted in localized spectro-temporal features. These features were then combined to cover a wide range of frequencies and temporal ranges. Spectro-temporal processing based on a 2D discrete cosine transform (DCT) was analyzed by Ezzat et al. (2007). The 2D-DCT was applied to patches of the short-time Fourier transform. By using only lower coefficients as basis for ASR features, relevant information including spectro-temporal patterns were extracted from speech. Despite the different approaches in these studies, spectro-temporal features were found to improve the baseline recognizers in stream combination experiments by approximately 20-30 %.

Even though the features described so far have the potential of reducing the human-machine gap in ASR discussed above for extrinsic variations (i.e., speech-in-noise), it is unclear if they show the same potential for intrinsic variations. Both properties would be a necessary prerequisite for including spectro-temporal features in advanced auditory models for human speech perception as well as ASR systems in order to close the human-machine performance gap. This study is based on the work by Kleinschmidt et al., and focuses on the robustness against the variability in spoken language. It was investigated if the explicit use of spectro-temporal information helps to increase overall robustness against extrinsic and intrinsic factors. Additionally, we report on complementary information of MFCCs and spectro-temporal features, and on the theoretical and practical improvements resulting from a combination of feature types.

4.1 Feature types

4.1.1 Spectro-temporal Gabor features

Gabor features are calculated by processing a spectro-temporal representation of the input signal with a number of 2-D modulation filters. The filtering is performed by correlation over time of each input frequency channel with the corresponding part of the Gabor function (centered on the current frame and desired frequency channel) and a subsequent summation over frequency. This yields one output value per frame per filter and is equivalent to a 2-D correlation of the input representation with the complete filter function and a subsequent selection of the desired frequency channel of the output. In this study, log mel-spectrograms serve as input features for the feature extraction. This was chosen for its widespread use in ASR and because the logarithmic compression and mel-frequency scale may be considered a very simple model of peripheral auditory processing. Even though features from a more sophisticated auditory model could have been used for spectral decomposition and temporal envelope compression (such as, e.g., the perception model used by Tchorz and Kollmeier (1999)) the usage of the standard preprocessing stage allows for a better separation of the observed effects between (temporal and spectral) preprocessing and the spectro-temporal feature extraction which is of primary interest here.

The two-dimensional complex Gabor function $G(n,k)$ is defined as the product of a truncated Gaussian envelope $g(n,k)$ and the complex sinusoidal function $s(n,k)$. Alternatively, the filter can be designed as the product of a Hanning envelope $h(n,k)$ and $s(n,k)$, which was shown to result in improved filter characteristics and improved ASR scores (Meyer and Kollmeier, 2008). In this study we therefore use modified Gabor filters with a Hanning envelope. Examples of the real part of a 2-D filter and for a 1-D filter are shown in Fig. 4.2.

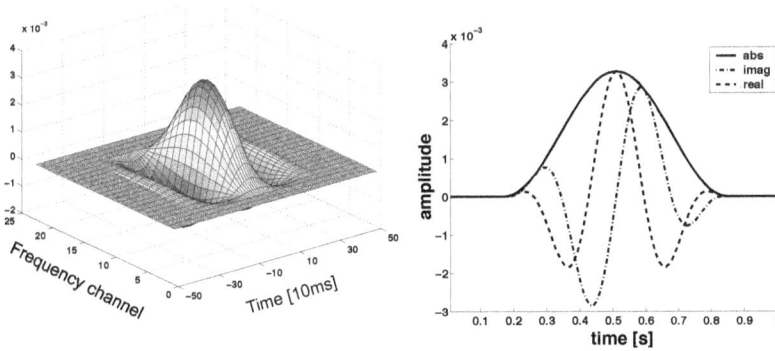

FIG. 4.2 *Illustration of 1- and 2-dimensional filter prototypes for spectro-temporal filters. In the left panel, the real part of complex 2D impulse responses is depicted. The right panel shows real and imaginary parts as well as envelope of a 1D-filters, corresponding to a cross section of a two dimensional filter.*

The envelope width is defined by the window lengths W_n and W_k, while the periodicity is defined by the radian frequencies ω_n and ω_k with n and k denoting the time and frequency index, respectively. The two independent parameters ω_n and ω_k allow the Gabor function to be tuned to particular directions of spectro-temporal modulation, including *diagonal* modulations. Further parameters are the centers of mass of the envelope in time and frequency n_0 and k_0. In this notation, the Hanning envelope *h(n,k)* is defined as

$$h(n, k) = 0.5 \; + \; 0.5 \cdot \cos\left(\frac{2\pi(n - n_0)}{W_n + 1}\right) \cdot \cos\left(\frac{2\pi(k - k_0)}{W_k + 1}\right).$$

and the complex sinusoid *s(n,k)* as

$$s(n, k) = \exp\left[i\omega_n(n - n_0) + i\omega_k(k - k_0)\right].$$

The envelope width is chosen depending on the modulation frequency ω_x, (with $x = k$ or $x = n$) respective the corresponding period T_x, either with a fixed ratio $v_x = T_x \,/\, 2W_x = 1$ to obtain a 2D wavelet prototype or by allowing a certain range $v_x = 1...3$ with individual values for T_x being optimized in the automatic feature selection process. For time dependent features, n_0 is set to the current frame, leaving k_0, ω_k and ω_n as free parameters. From the complex results of the filter operation, real-valued features are obtained by using the real, imaginary or absolute part only. In this case, the overall DC bias was removed from the template. The magnitude of the complex output can also be used. Special cases are purely temporal filters ($\omega_k = 0$) and purely spectral filters *($\omega_n = 0$)*. In these cases, W_x replaces $\omega_x = 0$ as a free parameter, denoting the extent of the filter, perpendicular to its direction of modulation.

Feature set optimization

In order to apply Gabor filters to the problem of speech recognition, parameter sets from a large number of possible combinations need to be determined[1]. Feature set optimization is carried out by a modified version of a Feature-finding Neural Network (FFNN). It consists of a linear single-layer perceptron in conjunction with an

---

[1]This issue may be solved implicitly by automatic learning in neural networks with a spectrogram input and long time windows of e.g. 1s. However, this is computationally expensive and prone to overfitting, as it requires large amounts of training data, which are also often unavailable. By putting further constraints on the spectro-temporal patterns, the number of free parameters can be decreased by several orders of magnitude. This is the case when a specific analytical function, such as the Gabor function, is explicitly demanded. This approach narrows the search to a certain sub-set and thereby some important features might be ignored. However, neurophysiological and psychoacoustical knowledge can be exploited for the choice of the prototype, as is done here.

optimization rule for the feature set (Gramss and Strube, 1990). The linear classifier guarantees fast training, which is necessary because in this wrapper method for feature selection the importance of each feature is evaluated by the increase of rms classification error after its removal from the set. This 'substitution rule' method (Gramss, 1991) requires iterative re-training of the classifier and replacing the least relevant feature in the set with a randomly drawn new one. When the filter set is optimized with a database containing isolated words without phoneme labels, a temporal integration of features is carried out by simple summation of the feature vectors over the whole utterance. This results in one feature vector per utterance as required for the linear net. The FFNN approach has been successfully applied to digit recognition in combination with Gabor features in the past (Kleinschmidt, 2002; Kleinschmidt and Gelbart, 2002).

The Gabor filter set used in this study was obtained by using the FFNN with the ZIFKOM German digit data, which contains single digit utterances spoken by 100 female and 100 male speakers. It was equally split into a training and test set with noises added as proposed in the AURORA 2 framework. Temporal and spectral modulation frequencies for the filters were randomly chosen in an interval from 2 to 50 Hz and 0.06 to 0.5 cycles/octave, respectively. Boundary conditions for the spectral extent of the filter guaranteed that even at low modulation frequencies the filters did not exceed 23 frequency channels or 101 time frames (corresponding to 1s filter length). The filter set contained 80 filter functions; the 15 filters which resulted in being most relevant for the classification of the speech data are shown in Fig. 4.3.

Non-linear transformation

The original 80-dimensional filter output was processed by a Tandem system (Hermansky et al., 2000) as shown in Fig. 4.4: In a first step, the feature vectors were online normalized and combined with delta and double-delta derivatives before using them as input to a non-linear neural net (or multi-layer perceptron (MLP)). The MLP was provided by the QuickNet software package (http://www.icsi.berkeley.edu) and had 80N, 1000 and 56 neurons in input, hidden and output layer, respectively. It was trained on the TIMIT phone-labeled database with artificially added noise. The resulting posteriors were decorrelated using a principal component analysis (PCA) which yields 56-dimensional, decorrelated feature vectors. These vectors are used as input features to a Hidden Markov model (see Section 4.2.2).

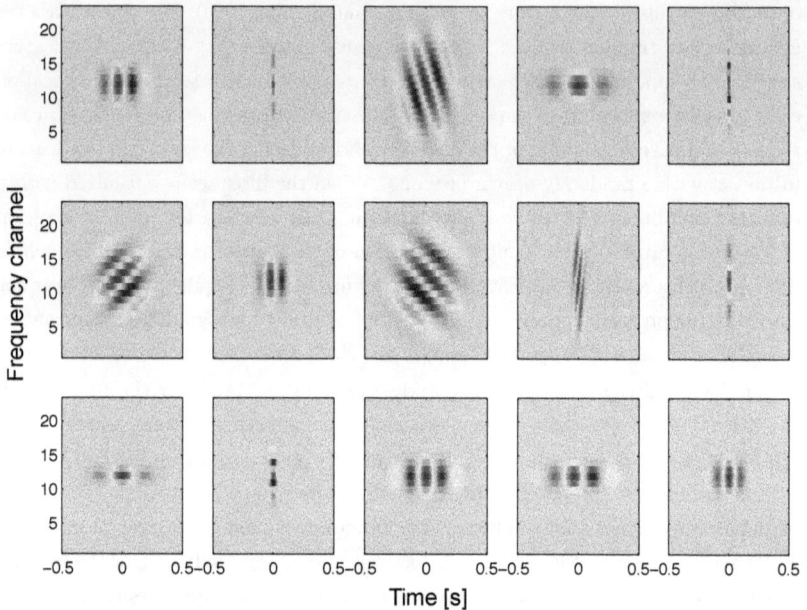

FIG. 4.3 *Gabor filter functions obtained with the Feature Finding Neural Network. The figure shows the 15 most relevant filters from a set with a total of 80 filters. About 60 % of the filters had a spectro-temporal structure, while 30 % were purely spectral or temporal, respectively.*

4.1.2 MFCC features

Mel-frequency cepstral coefficients (MFCCs) have been chosen as baseline for this series of experiments. For the computation of MFCCs (Davis and Mermelstein, 1980), a pre-emphasis is applied to the signal before calculating the smoothed short-time Fourier transform (STFT). Each frame is then processed by a mel-filterbank (which approximates the response of the human ear), compressed with the logarithm and transformed to cepstral parameters using an inverse discrete cosine transformation. By selecting the lower cepstral coefficients, only the coarse spectral structure is retained. This processing results in mostly decorrelated features.

For the presented experiments, MFCC features were calculated using the rastamat

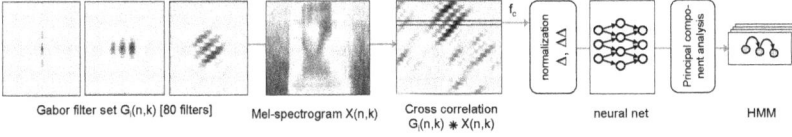

Gabor filter set G,(n,k) [80 filters] Mel-spectrogram X(n,k) Cross correlation G,(n,k) ∗ X(n,k) neural net HMM

FIG. 4.4 *Gabor features are calculated by correlation of each filter with a mel-spectrogram and subsequent selection of the center frequency f_c associated with each filter. This results in 80-dimensional vectors, which are processed with a non-linear neural net, a principal component analysis and a hidden Markov model. Gabor functions on the left are examples of purely temporal, spectral and spectro-temporal filters. The cross-correlation in this example was obtained with a spectro-temporal filter that emphasizes the diagonal transient.*

Matlab toolbox (Ellis, 2003) with parameters that resemble feature extraction from the HTK software (Young et al., 1995), i.e. the filter bank used 20 frequency channels; the 13-dimensional features were concatenated with delta and acceleration coefficients. Signals with 16 kHz bandwidth were used as input to the front-ends.

4.2 Methods

4.2.1 Speech databases, training and test sets

The robustness of ASR features against extrinsic variations, i.e., additive noise or channel distortions is often assessed by the performance loss produced by mismatches between training and test noise types or SNRs. Similarly, the robustness against intrinsic variations may be evaluated by training the recognizer on normally spoken utterances and testing it on utterances that cover a wider range of variabilities. In this work, two databases are used for ASR experiments to cover both aspects of variability.

AURORA 2 database

The AURORA 2 framework was used to assess the impact of additive noise sources. The database contains strings of connected digits from the TIDigits database (Leonard, 1984) to which various noise types were added at SNRs ranging from -5 dB to 20 dB in 5 dB-steps. The framework provides two training modes: 'Multi-condition' refers to training the recognizer with clean and noisy signals, where four noise types are used (suburban train, crowd of people (babble), car and exhibition hall). For 'clean condition' training, only utterances without additional noise have been employed.

The test set covers eight noise types at SNRs from -5 dB to 20 dB, as well as clean speech. Four of these noises are the same as for multi-condition training, while the remaining noises (restaurant, street, airport and train station) are not used during training. Therefore, the effect of matched vs. mismatched test and training can be investigated. The test set also includes speech signals filtered with a telephone bandpass characteristic before applying the noises suburban train and street, taking channel transmission effects into account.

In order to evaluate the robustness of a system, results for the clean trained HMM are of special interest, as the HMM models do not contain any specific information about possible distortions in this case. Therefore, the scores obtained with this training mode are a good measure for the invariance of features against the noise types in the test set.

Oldenburg Logatome Corpus

The Oldenburg Logatome Corpus (OLLO) is a database that was recorded for speech intelligibility tests with human listeners and for experiments with automatic classifiers (Wesker et al., 2005). It consists of non-sense utterances or logatomes, i.e. words without semantic meaning which comply with phonetic and phonotactic rules. The logatomes are composed of triplets of vowels (V) and consonants (C), with the outer phonemes being identical. 50 speakers recorded 70 VCVs and 80 CVCs with different speaking styles, efforts and speaking rates, thus enabling an analysis of the effect of such *intrinsic* variations of speech. During the recordings, participants were asked to speak each logatome either normally or in one of five variations. The properties of the database are listed in Table 4.1. For details on the OLLO corpus, the reader is referred to (Wesker et al., 2005).

For the ASR experiments in this study, subsets of the OLLO database were selected for training and test of the recognizer (Table 4.1). The variabilities fast and slow speaking rate, high and low speaking effort (conditions 'loud' and 'soft'), and condition 'question' which refers to utterances with rising pitch were equally distributed in this selection. Additionally, normally spoken utterances were included as reference condition. The ASR task was to recognize one of 14 middle consonants or one of 10

No. of different VCVs	70 (five outer vowels (/a/, /ɛ/, /ɪ/, /ɔ/, /ʊ/) combined with 14 central consonants (/b/, /d/, /f/, /g/, /k/, /l/, /m/, /n/, /p/, /s/, /ʃ/, /t/, /v/, /ts/))
No. of different VCVs	80 (eight outer consonants (/b/, /d/, /f/, /g/, /k/, /p/, /s/, /t/) combined with 10 central vowels (/a/, /ɛ/, /ɪ/, /ɔ/, /ʊ/, /aː/, /e/, /i/, /o/, /u/))
No. of different logatomes	150
No. of speaking styles	5 (fast, slow, loud, soft, question) + ref. condition 'normal'
No. of speakers in training set	6 (3 male, 3 female, no dialect)
No. of speakers in test set	4 (2 male, 2 female, no dialect, speaker ids {1, 2, 6, 8})

TABLE 4.1 *Properties of the Oldenburg Logatome database and the training and test sets used for the ASR experiments.*

central vowels. The use of a phoneme recognition task allows for an analysis of the recognition of phonemic-articulatory features, such as voicing or the place and manner of articulation to gain some insight into which properties of speech sounds result in correct and false classification.

Utterances of the OLLO database from three male and three female German talkers without dialect served as training data, logatomes from the four remaining speakers without dialect were used for the test. The chosen segmentation of the corpus results in a speaker- and gender-independent ASR system. While the training set contained only normally spoken logatomes, the test set additionally contained utterances with the aforementioned variations (conditions 'fast', 'slow', 'loud', 'soft', 'question').

The training and test was carried out with noisy signals for which a speech-shaped stationary noise (Dreschler et al., 1999) was added to the utterances at SNRs ranging from -10 to 10 dB in 5 dB-steps. Since the focus of this experiment was on intrinsic variations, the same SNR was chosen for training and test. The SNR was calculated by relating the root-mean-square (rms) value of the speech segments of each audio signal and the rms value of the masking noise of equal length. A simple voice detection algorithm based on an energy criterion was used to extract connected speech segments. Additionally, the classifier was trained and tested with clean speech.

4.2.2 Automatic recognizers

HTK baseline recognition system

Gabor and MFCC features were used to train and test recognition systems based on Hidden Markov models (HMM), implemented in the HMM toolkit (Young et al., 1995). For experiments with the AURORA 2 database, the classifier was configured according to (Hirsch and Pearce, 2000), i.e. the HMM used 16 states per word and three Gaussian mixtures per state, which are connected by a left-right-model that not allows for skipping states. For experiments with the Oldenburg Logatome corpus, the task was defined as recognition of the central phoneme in the CVCs and VCVs, mimicking earlier experiments with human listeners based on the OLLO corpus (Meyer and Wesker, 2006). Logatomes with the same outer phoneme were used to train and test single HMMs (based on HTK) which were subsequently used to classify the central phoneme in CVCs and VCVs, i.e., confusion occured only for central phonemes. Note that in this test setup, confusions between the consonant and the vowel group cannot occur. The HTK was configured with three states per phoneme and eight mixtures per state.

Philips Continuous ASR system

Additionally, the performance of Gabor features vs. MFCCs was tested using a more advanced recognition system, i.e. the Philips Continuous ASR system (Lieb and Fischer, 2002). This classifier was chosen for two reasons: First, it was investigated if Gabor features can increase performance in a recognition system that incorporates denoising techniques as well as methods to improve auditory modeling such as discriminative training for HMMs. Second, the Philips ASR system provides methods to combine feature streams that were used for an analysis regarding feature complementarity of purely spectral and spectro-temporal features, as described in Section 4.3.4.

The feature extraction stage is based on MFCCs (12 cepstral coefficients with delta features which yields 24-dim. feature vectors) and an HMM classifier, and combines feature extraction techniques such as non-linear spectral subtraction, noise-masking or linear discriminant analysis (LDA) and classification based on discriminative training. Gabor and MFCC features were used as input to the recognizer both individually and

Articulatory feature	Feature values	Corresponding phonemes
Place	Bilabial	/p/, /b/, /m/
	Alveolar	/f/, /v/
	Labiodental	/t/, /d/, /n/, /s/, /ts/, /l/
	Palato-Alveolar	/ʃ/
	Velar	/k/, /g/
Manner	Plosive	/p/, /t/, /k/, /b/, /d/, /g/
	Nasal	/n/, /m/
	Fricative	/s/, /f/, /v/, /ʃ/, /ts/
	Lat. Approx.	/l/
Voicing	Voiced	/b/, /d/, /g/, /v/, /n/, /m/, /l/
	Unvoiced	/p/, /t/, /k/, /s/, /f/, /ʃ/, /ts/
Backness	Back	/ɔ/, /ʊ/, /o/, /u/
	Front	/a/, /ɛ/, /ɪ/, /aː/, /e/, /i/
Height	Closed	/ɪ/, /ʊ/, /i/, /u/
	Close-mid	/e/, /o/
	Open-mid	/ɛ/, /ɔ/
	Open	/a/, /aː/

TABLE 4.2 *Articulatory features, their feature values, and the phonemes that correspond to a specific feature value (based on the International Phonetic Alphabet proposed by the International Phonetic Association)*

with a combination of feature streams. As for the experiments based on HTK, the training and test sets as proposed in the Aurora 2 framework were used.

4.2.3 Articulatory features and transmitted information

The acoustic cues important for consonant identification are analyzed by decomposing consonants into their articulatory features (AFs). This method of data analysis was proposed by Miller and Nicely (1955) who used five linguistic or articulatory features to group speech stimuli, i.e., voicing, nasality, affrication, duration, place of articulation. The features of nasality and affrication may be combined into one feature 'manner of articulation' with three possible feature values (stop, nasal or fricative) which refers to the mode of articulatory production. The confusion analysis presented in this study is based on AFs with values as shown in Table 4.2.

These features originate from the set defined by (Jacobsen et al., 1952); their values are based on the International Phonetic Alphabet (Handbook, 1999). The features 'voicing', 'place of articulation' and 'manner of articulation' are associated with consonant phonemes, while 'backness' and 'height' were calculated from vowel confusions.

Values in the articulatory CM do not solely depend on the information transmission associated with a particular feature and stimulus condition but also on the entropy of feature values which, e.g., is reflected by the respective chance performance and/or response bias. To correct for this effect, the amount of transmitted information was computed by measuring the relationship between the probability distribution p_i of a specific stimulus x and the response frequency (or probability) distribution p_j, of the respective response category y. The information transmission (or mutual information) $T(x,y)$ is computed using the expression

$$T(x, y) = -\sum_{i,j} p_{ij} \log \frac{p_i p_j}{p_{ij}}$$

with the input variable x and the output variable y, each having the possible values i = 1, 2, ..., k and j = 1, 2, ..., m, respectively, with the corresponding probabilities p_i, p_j, and the joint probability p_{ij}. The indices i and j refer to the index in the phoneme confusion matrix associated with the 24 central phonemes of the OLLO database. The complete confusion matrix is used to compute the global information transmission by the consonants or vowels in the OLLO recognition task. Moreover, the phoneme confusion matrix is transformed into the feature confusion matrix for each of the respective features listed in Table 4.2 that has a much lower dimensionality. The indices i and j refer to the index in the feature confusion matrix with the elements p_{ij}. The probabilities p_i and p_j are the *a-priori* and *a-posteriori* probabilities for the stimuli. Hence, determining $T(x,y)$ from the confusion matrices for each of the phonetic features can be used to assess the information transmission for each AF. Since the logarithm is taken to the base 2, $T(x,y)$ is a measure of how many bits are given by the output to specify the information in the input. To make the transmitted information independent from the already existent information in the input, we report the relative information transmission $T_r = T(x, y)/H(x)$ with the source entropy $H(x) = \sum_i p_i \log(p_i)$ (Miller and Nicely, 1955).

4.3 Results

This section is structured as follows: First, the results for the experiments aiming at robustness against extrinsic variations are reported. The effect of *intrinsic* variations and the analysis with articulatory features is presented in Sections 4.3.2 and 4.3.3, respectively; the detailed results of these experiments are reported in Tables 4.4 and 4.5. Complementary information of spectral and spectro-temporal features is discussed in Section 4.3.4.

4.3.1 Effect of extrinsic variations

On the AURORA 2 task with various additive noise conditions, Gabor features improved the baseline for all noise types as shown in Table 4.3. Additionally, we show

	Subway	Babble	Car	Exhibition	Restaurant	Street	Airport	Station	Subway M	Street M	average
Multi cond.											
MFCC	89.1	88.4	86.8	88.0	86.6	87.8	88.3	86.2	83.5	85.7	87.0
Gabor	89.9	89.1	88.9	89.3	87.2	88.7	89.6	87.8	88.1	87.3	88.6
Rel. Red. WER	7.3	5.9	16.5	11.4	4.8	8.0	10.8	11.1	28.1	11.1	11.5
MFCC		88.1				87.2				84.6	
Gabor		89.3				88.3				87.7	
Rel. Red. WER		10.5				8.6				20.2	
Clean cond.											
MFCC	66.7	47.8	58.1	62.4	50.1	60.7	49.6	53.1	65.3	66.7	58.1
Gabor	86.1	79.1	84.7	83.9	75.4	83.4	80.4	82.5	85.5	82.7	82.4
Rel. Red. WER	58.3	60.0	63.6	57.2	50.7	57.7	61.1	62.7	58.3	48.1	57.8
MFCC		58.7				53.4				66.0	
Gabor		83.5				80.4				84.1	
Rel. Red. WER		59.8				58.1				53.2	

TABLE 4.3 *Recognition scores and relative reduction of word errors for the AURORA 2 digit recognition task. The training was carried out either with clean speech, or with a speech mixed with various noise types ('multi'). Tests were always performed using using a mixture of noisy and clean signals.*

the reduction in WER, which are commonly reported for AURORA 2. On average, errors with Gabor features were reduced by 11.5 % relative for multi-condition training. When the recognizer is trained with clean utterances and tested with a variety of noise types the difference between the feature types becomes more noticeable with a relative reduction of 57.8 % in WER.

Gabors consistently outperform MFCCs for noise types which are used in multi-condition training (first four noise types in Table 4.3), as well as for noises not being used for the training (noises 5-8), and noisy signals which have been filtered with realistic frequency characteristics ('Subway M' and 'Street M'). The average benefit is consistent over these conditions, i.e., Gabor features have a similar sensitivity against mismatches of the employed training noises as MFCCs.

4.3.2 Effect of intrinsic variations

ASR phoneme recognition rates depending on speech intrinsic variations are shown in Tables 4.4 and 4.5 for MFCC and Gabor features. Gabor features that were used as direct input to the HMM (i.e., the non-linear transformation with the neural net as described in Section 4.1.1 was omitted) produced scores between MFCC and non-linearly transformed Gabor features and are not shown in the table.

The overall performance with matched training and test conditions is similar for cepstral and Gabor features: When averaging over all SNRs and variabilities, the phoneme accuracy is 51.0 % (MFCCs) and 53.3. % (Gabors). Intrinsic variations degrade ASR performance compared to the reference condition for both feature types. The performance drop averaged over all SNRs (including SNRs -10 dB and 10 dB) is 13.7 and 15.1 % absolute for MFCCs and Gabor features, respectively. The relative increase in terms of word error rate is 26.2 % and 30.4 %. Rather large differences between the ASR feature types are observed for the conditions 'loud' and 'question': When clean utterances are used for training and test, MFCCs produce 35 % more errors than spectro-temporal features. In average, Gabor features were found to be less sensitive to changes in speaking effort ('loud' and 'soft') and style ('question') than MFCCs (cf. average values in Tables 4.4 and 4.5). On the other hand, spectro-temporal features are more affected by variations of speaking rate ('fast' and 'slow'). These differences are analyzed based on confusions of articulatory features (Section 4.3).

SNR	Rec. rate	Consonant	Voicing	Place	Manner	Vowels	Backness	Height

Fast speaking rate, avg. rec. rate (all SNRs): MFCC: 50.5, Gabor 50.5

	SNR	Rec. rate	Consonant	Voicing	Place	Manner	Vowels	Backness	Height
MFCC	-5	37.6	20.9	8.4	16.7	8.7	36.0	39.7	31.9
Gabor	-5	41.4	9.2	1.6	9.5	1.4	49.9	56.9	43.3
MFCC	0	53.2	33.4	29.1	27.6	23.4	54.8	69.5	44.3
Gabor	0	52.1	18.7	10.8	17.6	10.4	61.1	76.3	52.7
MFCC	5	62.7	47.4	35.6	42.4	39.7	59.8	78.6	50.9
Gabor	5	58.2	23.9	16.5	19.2	16.1	63.5	81.3	53.3
MFCC	Clean	68.3	59.8	49.4	57.2	55.5	63.1	86.8	55.5
Gabor	Clean	65.6	48.0	34.1	40.3	45.0	56.9	82.8	46.4

Slow speaking rate, avg. rec. rate (all SNRs): MFCC: 56.6, Gabor 52.9

	SNR	Rec. rate	Consonant	Voicing	Place	Manner	Vowels	Backness	Height
MFCC	-5	37.7	25.0	20.5	18.6	15.6	31.8	30.5	27.9
Gabor	-5	44.8	10.4	3.8	10.2	2.7	47.6	42.0	46.5
MFCC	0	61.7	45.2	47.4	36.2	34.3	62.5	72.6	56.8
Gabor	0	56.1	26.0	20.4	22.0	20.5	69.2	66.4	60.8
MFCC	5	72.1	63.0	66.6	52.8	60.7	69.3	85.5	62.8
Gabor	5	62.2	31.9	28.7	25.5	28.8	72.1	78.0	63.0
MFCC	Clean	75.2	70.7	74.4	62.6	67.6	68.5	93.1	63.6
Gabor	Clean	69.6	69.0	72.4	55.9	66.9	60.4	78.3	48.2

Loud speaking style, avg. rec. rate (all SNRs): MFCC: 44.8, Gabor 49.1

	SNR	Rec. rate	Consonant	Voicing	Place	Manner	Vowels	Backness	Height
MFCC	-5	37.6	15.6	6.5	10.7	5.5	38.7	42.9	31.8
Gabor	-5	40.1	7.6	4.5	5.3	3.4	49.0	43.8	39.7
MFCC	0	50.0	26.8	14.8	19.9	13.4	53.8	58.8	44.3
Gabor	0	50.3	18.8	19.3	13.1	12.3	60.8	62.7	47.2
MFCC	5	54.3	32.4	20.3	28.4	19.0	55.4	61.4	44.0
Gabor	5	55.2	28.2	35.1	21.1	20.3	64.4	63.3	51.9
MFCC	Clean	55.9	43.5	36.9	35.8	34.4	55.0	71.2	45.4
Gabor	Clean	67.3	62.5	67.6	48.4	60.7	62.1	74.6	48.1

TABLE 4.4 *ASR recognition rates for high and low speaking rate and increased speaking effort, obtained with MFCC and Gabor features. A speech-shaped masking noise was used in training and test. Additionally, the relative transmitted information for each experimental condition is presented. Average values were obtained by averaging over SNR conditions, including SNRs of -10 and 10dB, which are not shown in the table.*

	SNR	Rec. rate	Consonant	Voicing	Place	Manner	Vowels	Backness	Height
Soft speaking style, avg. rec. rate (all SNRs): MFCC: 46.0, Gabor 50.0									
MFCC	-5	27.0	20.0	14.0	13.0	10.8	14.5	13.4	10.6
Gabor	-5	37.5	11.7	7.9	9.4	4.9	29.7	24.5	27.0
MFCC	0	47.2	36.4	38.2	23.9	29.6	39.1	48.1	31.4
Gabor	0	51.1	24.3	26.3	18.7	18.2	53.5	58.3	40.2
MFCC	5	59.1	49.1	51.5	39.8	44.6	51.9	68.5	44.1
Gabor	5	61.8	35.9	43.1	25.8	34.7	59.7	68.1	42.8
MFCC	Clean	67.0	65.5	61.5	62.3	57.5	60.0	86.1	51.1
Gabor	Clean	66.4	67.8	64.9	60.6	64.6	56.0	77.9	41.2

Condition 'Question', avg. rec. rate (all SNRs): MFCC: 45.7, Gabor 50.3									
MFCC	-5	33.6	22.9	16.7	17.9	13.2	27.3	30.4	24.7
Gabor	-5	37.5	9.0	3.1	9.2	2.3	46.8	45.5	43.0
MFCC	0	53.1	32.5	33.5	24.5	24.2	52.5	67.2	43.4
Gabor	0	50.4	22.8	24.0	15.8	20.9	60.9	65.1	52.5
MFCC	5	56.2	41.8	36.6	32.2	41.6	53.6	73.7	44.5
Gabor	5	58.2	28.8	38.4	19.6	24.2	67.8	76.9	58.7
MFCC	Clean	59.2	50.1	50.2	44.8	39.5	56.8	80.3	48.8
Gabor	Clean	70.6	73.1	68.1	68.7	74.2	59.3	80.8	46.2

Normal speaking style, avg. rec. rate (all SNRs): MFCC: 62.4, Gabor 65.6									
MFCC	-5	46.4	27.1	17.0	23.3	17.0	41.4	43.6	38.2
Gabor	-5	56.2	16.7	15.3	14.7	7.4	60.1	66.0	53.8
MFCC	0	70.2	50.2	50.5	43.0	40.8	68.7	79.9	61.4
Gabor	0	69.3	41.6	47.3	35.0	36.3	72.9	80.5	64.7
MFCC	5	76.2	62.8	62.0	53.2	58.0	73.9	84.7	66.6
Gabor	5	75.9	52.5	64.6	45.5	47.1	75.5	80.0	66.4
MFCC	Clean	78.0	70.7	71.9	64.4	63.3	70.9	94.1	66.4
Gabor	Clean	78.6	81.8	82.9	76.4	83.2	70.3	85.8	59.5

TABLE 4.5 *ASR recognition rates for low speaking effort, logatomes spoken with rising pitch, and the reference condition. See the caption of Table 4.4 for details.*

The performance degradation caused by intrinsic variations can be compared to the degradation caused by additive noise. Fig. 4.5 shows the relative increase of phoneme recognition error for both feature types. The relative increase in each panel is related to

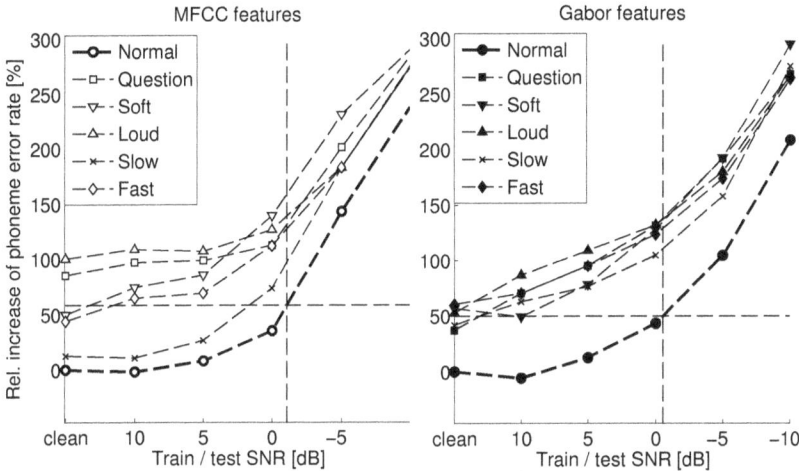

FIG. 4.5 *Relative increase of word error rate resulting from higher masking level and speech intrinsic variations for two ASR feature types, depending on the SNR used for training and test. The horizontal dashed line denotes the average increase of error E_V induced by intrinsic variability for clean utterances. The vertical line highlights the SNR at which the error of normally spoken utterances reaches E_V.*

normally spoken utterances without noise. When the recognizer is trained and tested with clean speech, changes of speaking style and effort result in an average increase of 55.5 % and 50.0 % for MFCC and Gabor features, respectively. The same overall degradation is caused by noise being added at approximately 0 dB for both features types.

Although the average reduction in accuracy is similar for both feature types, the variance of differences caused by intrinsic variations are larger for MFCCs than for Gabor features: For example, changes in speaking rate have a relatively small effect on MFCCs with a relative increase in error of 13 % for condition 'slow'. On the other hand, loud speaking style results in an increase of errors by a factor of two. With degradations between 37 % ('question') and 61 % ('fast'), the fluctuations observed for Gabor features are much smaller.

4.3.3 Articulatory features and information transmission

The relative transmitted information for articulatory features for normal speaking style is shown in Fig. 4.6 for two training and test conditions. The results for consonants and

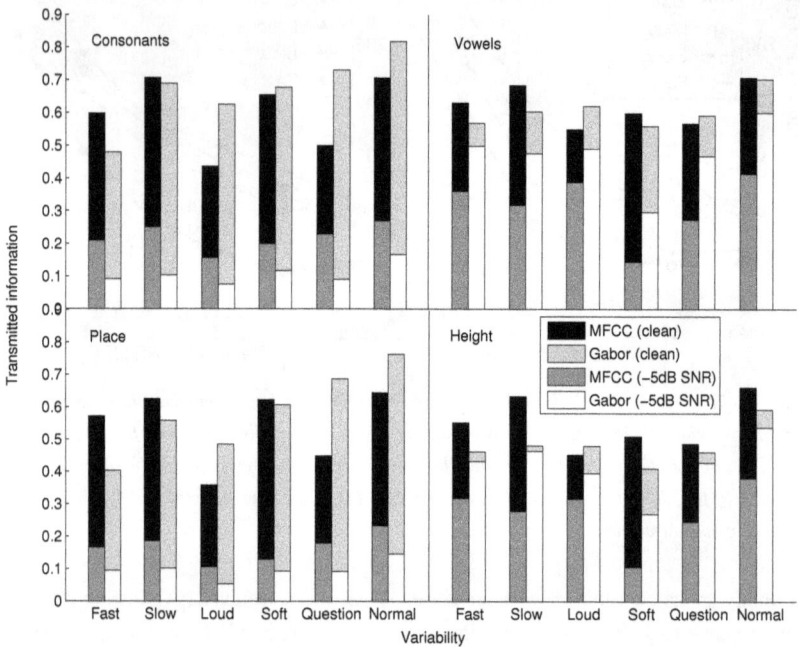

FIG. 4.6 *Relative transmitted information T_r for MFCC and spectro-temporal features for various articulatory features for two training and test conditions (clean and -5 dB SNR) for normal speaking style. The vertical line separates features associated with consonants (left) and vowels (right).*

vowels were derived directly from the corresponding phoneme confusion matrix. For clean speech, the recognition rates of consonants (and AFs associated with consonants) are 20.0 % higher in average with spectro-temporal features than for MFCCs. Overall vowel recognition is almost identical, but the AFs 'backness' and 'height' show higher scores for MFCCs. The opposite is true at low SNRs, where vowels seem to be better represented by Gabor features, and AFs corresponding to consonants are relatively high for MFCCs.

The transmitted information depending on intrinsic variations is presented in Fig. 4.7 for consonants and vowels, as well as for the articulatory features height and place of confusion. The scores shown in the figure depend on two parameters, i.e., the

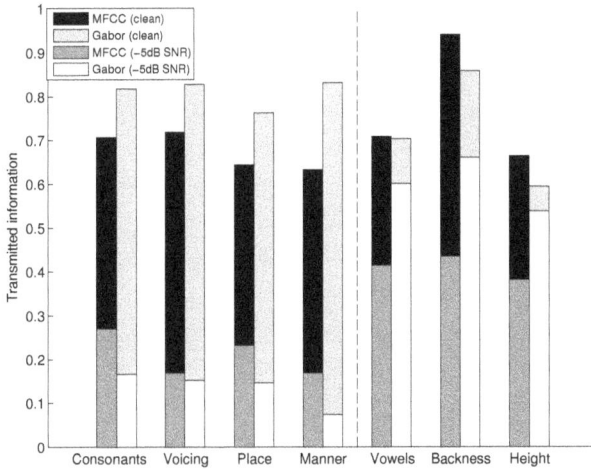

FIG. 4.7 *Transmitted information for MFCC and Gabor features, articulatory features and speech-intrinsic variabilities for two noise conditions.*

SNR used for training and test, and intrinsic variation. For Gabor features, the degradation of performance for changed speaking rate (cf. average values in Table 4.4) is reflected in the recognition of consonants and the AF 'place of articulation', while vowel recognition is not as strong influenced by fast and slow speaking style. In case of cepstral coefficients, the degraded performance for slow speaking rate is mainly caused by vowel-associated confusions, whereas for loud speaking style the performance loss can be contributed to the degradation of consonant features.

Fig. 4.5 showed that at 0 dB the performance for clearly spoken utterances is approximately the same as for speech with varying speaking rate and style. In order to analyze if this is true on a more 'microscopic' level (i.e. if the same applies for confusions of AFs of phonemes), we compared the articulatory features of both conditions (condition 'normal' at 0 dB vs. the average over all variabilities (excluding 'normal') for clean speech). The results (Fig. 4.8) show that the recognizer is affected differently in the presence of extrinsic and intrinsic variations: Adding additive noise results in degraded scores for consonants and consonant-associated features, whereas intrinsic variations affected vowel recognition.

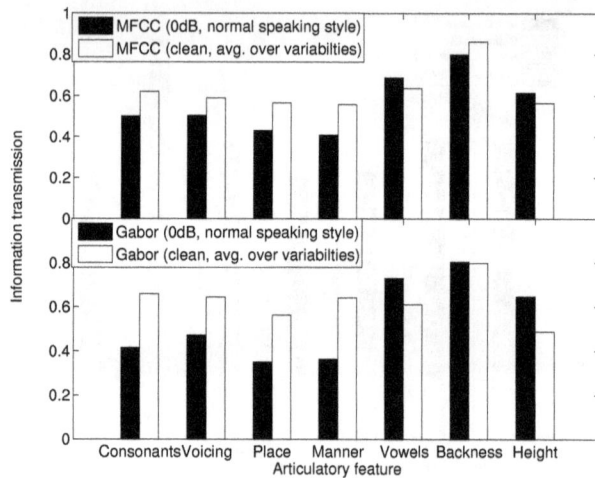

FIG. 4.8 *Comparison of conditions at which the same overall performance was found due to additive noise ('0 dB') and intrinsic variations ('clean, avg. over variabilities').*

4.3.4 Complementarity of spectral and spectro-temporal features

While the limitation to purely spectral information is a theoretical disadvantage of MFCCs, it is often difficult to achieve improvements for tuned ASR systems with completely new features. We therefore investigated if both feature types carry complementary information and if a combination of Gabor and MFCC features is a promising approach. For these experiments, we chose results obtained with the Philips continuous recognizer (Lieb and Fischer, 2002) with an improved feature extraction stage (cf.

	Word accuracy		
	Multi	Clean	Average
a) MFCCs	83.7	54.9	69.3
b) Denoised MFCCs	91.4	89.8	90.6
c) Gabor	89.7	81.2	85.4
d) Oracle	96.3	95.3	95.8
e) Gabor + Denoised MFCCs (b + c)	93.4	90.7	92.0

TABLE 4.6 *Word accuracies obtained with original and denoised MFCCs and Gabor features. Oracle results show the theoretical improvements that a perfect classifier with knowledge about which feature stream would perform best could achieve. The best real-world performance is obtained with a stream combination of MFCC and Gabor features processed by an MLP.*

Section 4.2.2). The recognition task was the same as for the HTK recognizer, i.e., digit classification within the AURORA 2 framework.

The intersection of misclassified digit tokens E from both systems was chosen as a measure for complementary information: $I_{err} = E_{Gabor} \cap E_{MFCC}$. The smaller I_{err} is, the smaller is the error rate of an (imaginary) perfect classifier that can use the MFCC or the Gabor feature information, and thus only produces an error if a digit was misclassified by *both* single-stream systems. A low error rate of such a perfect or 'oracle' system represents a high complementarity of feature streams. Insertions and deletions are included in I_{err} if an insertion or deletion occurs at the same position of the transcribed string of digits. The word accuracies of both feature types and the oracle system are shown in Table 4.6. Performance obtained with Gabors was between scores for denoised and original MFCC features. When denoised MFCCs are used as baseline, the perfect knowledge scenario decreases the error rates about 55 % relative.

These results motivated a combination of feature streams: Denoised MFCCs were concatenated with Gabor features and used to train and test the Philips recognizer, as described in Section 4.2.2. Before concatenation, Gabor features were reduced to 24 dimensions by selecting the first 24 components of the PCA-transformed feature vector (cf. Table 4.6). Adding MFCCs resulted in 48-dimensional vectors, which were transformed to 24-dimensional vectors using a linear discriminant analysis. Since all feature vectors that were compared had 24 components, the number of model parameters of the classifier was kept constant.

The result of the stream combination experiment is shown in Table 4.6 (row e):

The word accuracy was improved for clean and multi-condition training when using concatenated Gabor features and denoised MFCCs. The scores correspond to relative reductions of 16 % in average and 23 % for multi-condition training compared to denoised MFCCs. Compared to MFCCs without denoising, the average reduction in WER is over 70 %.

4.4 Discussion

4.4.1 Robustness of Gabor features against extrinsic variations

The comparison of spectro-temporal and MFCC features showed that Gabor features provide increased robustness against a wide range of noise sources. Improvements over the AURORA 2 baseline were found when the recognizer was trained on noisy utterances. The average reduction in relative word error was 35 % for the HTK recognizer and 47 % for the Philips Continuous ASR system compared to MFCC features.

The increased performance might be a result of the FFNN algorithm: Since the optimization of filter parameters is carried out on speech material, the (optimized) Gabor filters can be considered as matched filters for distinctive speech features. These filters appear as relatively robust against additive noise. In contrast to this, the spectral content of speech is well encoded by MFCC features which deliver good performance for tests with clean speech. However, this representation seems to be severely degraded in the presence of noise. It might be the spectro-temporal cues (which might be redundant for clean speech, but become more important at low SNRs) which cause the good robustness against extrinsic variations found in these experiments. Interestingly, the best performance with Gabor features were obtained with filter sets on German digit data, although one of the recognition tasks was the classification of English utterances. This indicates that Gabor filter sets might be suitable for a larger group of recognition tasks without the need to optimize a new filter set for each test condition.

In several physiological studies (Depireux et al., 2001; Qiu et al., 2003) it was reported that a large proportion of spectro-temporal receptive fields in the auditory cortex are separable, i.e., the STRFs can be expressed as the product of a spectral and a temporal function and do therefore not contain any 'true' spectro-temporal patterns. However, in our experiments with separable Gabor functions, we have so far not been able to improve the results compared to the non-separable Gabor functions which have been used in this study. This indicates that at least parts of the speech information that the (optimized) Gabor features from our set are matched to cannot be represented by a simple combination of spectral and temporal properties. Instead, a time-varying spectral content (resembling, for example, a transition in fundamental frequency or formant frequency) is specifically captured by some of the Gabor features employed here.

4.4.2 Effect of intrinsic variations

Intrinsic variations (speaking rate, style and effort) had a strong impact on ASR performance, with an overall degradation of approximately 50 % for phoneme recognition in clean speech (Fig. 4.5). Our analysis showed that Gabor features differ from MFCC features regarding sensitivity against intrinsic parameters: MFCC features were less sensitive against changes in speaking rate, while the overall recognition of speaking effort and style was improved with Gabor features. Thus, the usage of spectro-temporal features is not only beneficial for overall performance, but also results in different sensitivity against intrinsic variations, which could be utilized to increase robustness by combining properties of cepstral and Gabor features.

The reason for the higher error rates for fast spoken utterances might be that the optimization of the filter set was carried out on words that were spoken at normal speaking rate. Higher spectro-temporal modulation frequencies, which could be better suited to detect, e.g., formant transitions of speech at high speaking rate, may therefore not be included in the filter set. For purely spectral features, the adaptation to different rates of speech is performed in the back-end stage, whereas some of the timing information is included in the spectro-temporal features which are "frozen" in a certain word production speed used during learning. An adaptation of Gabor filters to other speaking rates could be performed by including utterances with fast and slow speaking rate (e.g., from the OLLO database) during filter selection.

The increase in WER due to intrinsic variations was compared to the increase due to additive noise (Fig. 4.5). The overall effect of the analyzed speaking style, effort and rate was approximately the same as for a stationary masker added at 0 dB SNR to clean signals. This result was obtained in a phoneme recognition task with matched ASR training and test. It remains to be seen if this result holds for other tasks as well (e.g., recognition of words or conversational speech) that require other speech databases with labels of such variations of speech. The analysis based on transmitted information showed that the type of error patterns differs for the described conditions: additive noise affected the consonant-associated features, presumably because consonants have less energy than vowels and are therefore masked by the stationary noise. This was not the case for intrinsic variations, for which the transmitted information of vowels and vowel features was affected more strongly. This may be caused by the stronger variations in the articulation of vowels due to an altered speaking style (such as, e.g., fast, slow, question, ...) as opposed to the consonants that are roughly articulated in the same way.

4.4.3 Interaction between ASR features and articulatory features

The analysis based on transmitted information of *clean* speech showed that consonants and the AFs 'voicing', 'place' and 'manner' are better recognized with Gabor features, while MFCCs had advantages for vowels and the vowel-AFs 'backness' and 'height'. For low SNRs, the opposite result was found (Fig. 4.6).

It seems that at high SNRs, the coding of spectral envelope performed by MFCCs is better suited and spectro-temporal cues are not required for vowel recognition, and that purely spectral coding of speech is sufficient in this case. As the SNR decreases, the robustness against additive noise becomes more salient. Gabor features encode the temporal modulation and local movement of speech energy typical for formant transients for vowels, which may result in a locally increased SNR and therefore enhanced performance. On the other hand, the good performance of MFCCs for consonants at low SNRs might be due to the presence of characteristic energy clusters that are separated in the frequency domain (e.g., high-frequency elements due to frication in combination with a low-frequency stop or formant maximum characteristic for manner and place of articulation) which can be favorably detected based on the spectral envelope. The fact that Gabors produced better consonant scores in clean speech might be due to the better representation of spectral fine structure and phoneme transitions, which are not included in cepstral coefficients, but used in Gabor features, and which were suggested to be included for ASR systems earlier (Dimitriadis et al., 2005; Scharenborg, 2007).

4.4.4 Complementarity of MFCC and Gabor features

The Gabor filter set was not designed with a combination with MFCCs in mind, but still resulted in an increase of performance when feature streams were concatenated (Table 4.6). Relative WERs were reduced both in a theoretical approach (55 %) as well as in a real-world scenario (16 %), which demonstrated the potential of this class of physiologically motivated features. However, this is not even halfway to the WER reduction observed for the oracle system, which motivates more advanced feature combination techniques, such as linear discriminant analysis or the combination of multiple neural nets. These findings are in line with results from related studies that analyze spectro-temporal features: When combining high-dimensional Gabor features with MFCCs in a multi-stream environment, an improvement in WER of 30 % was found (Zhu et al., 2005). Similarly, a combination of RASTA-PLP (Hermansky and Morgan, 1994) and spectro-temporal features was reported to lower ASR error rates by roughly 20 % (Heckmann et al., 2008).

Furthermore, the result suggests to include MFCCs in the feature selection process: The Gabor filter set with best performance exhibits 30 % purely spectral and temporal filters, respectively, while 40 % of the automatically defined filters are spectro-temporal. An inclusion of spectral features in the parameter definition process would presumably result in a shift away from spectro-temporal and purely temporal filters, thus increasing complementary information. Other candidates for features to be included during filter optimization are TRAPS features which account for the temporal dynamics of spoken language (Hermansky and Sharma, 1999).

Although the experiments based on the Oldenburg Logatome Corpus aimed at the effect of intrinsic variations, the robustness of the analyzed features types against *extrinsic* factors for that database are interesting with respect to complementarity: The data shows that consonant properties are well-recognized by Gabor features for clean speech (matched training and test), whereas MFCCs perform better for vowel AFs (and vice-versa for noisy speech). This result helps to understand why Gabor features are beneficial in a stream-combination experiment: Since the task defined in the AURORA 2 framework is to recognize digits in a wide range of SNRs and in clean speech, the different properties of feature types of spectral and spectro-temporal features help to increase overall robustness. We therefore argue that Gabor features and

MFCCs carry complementary information on different levels, which could be exploited in feature-stream experiments.

4.5 Conclusions

The most important findings from this study can be summarized as follows:

- Spectro-temporal Gabor features were found to be more robust than an MFCC-based classifier against a wide variety of extrinsic sources of variability: Small improvements were achieved when the classifier was trained and tested with a mixture of clean and noisy signals. When the training was performed with clean utterances, the reduction in word error rate was over 50 %. These results are in line with other studies that analyze spectro-temporal filters for ASR, and confirm that spectro-temporal information can help to increase robustness against noise.

- The presence of intrinsic variations such as speaking rate, style and effort severely degrades the performance of ASR. In acoustically optimal conditions, the average increase of errors was over 50 % for a phoneme recognition task. Purely spectral and spectro-temporal features were affected differently by these variabilities: While MFCCs were less susceptible to changes in speaking rate, the usage of spectro-temporal input for ASR resulted in performance above baseline for high and low speaking effort, as well as for utterances with rising pitch. This finding suggests a combination of spectral and spectro-temporal features in future experiments.

- The degradation due to intrinsic variations had a similar effect on overall phoneme recognition as a stationary, speech-shaped noise at approximately 0 dB SNR. This result was found both for cepstral and spectro-temporal features. However, the confusions of single phonemes and articulatory features clearly differed, thus demonstrating that intrinsic and extrinsic variations result in different microscopic confusions.

- The errors that occur with spectro-temporal features are genuinely different from MFCC features. An analysis regarding complementarity showed that a) different errors occur with each feature type on a digit recognition task and b) these features seem to carry complementary information which might be beneficial to consonant and vowel recognition both in clean and noisy speech. This motivated a combination of feature streams, which improved scores compared to a recognizer using denoised MFCCs as feature input

4.6 Acknowledgements

Supported by the DFG (SFB/TRR 31 'The active auditory system'; URL: http://www.uni-oldenburg.de/sfbtr31). The OLLO speech database has been developed as part of the EU DIVINES Project IST-2002-002034.

We thank Thomas Brand, Michael Kleinschmidt, David Gelbart, Alexander Fischer, and Jörg-Hendrik Bach for their contributions to this work. We also thank Frank Ohl, Max Happel, and Arne Meyer for providing the physiological data shown in Fig. 4.1.

5

Summary and general conclusions

This thesis presents an analysis of differences between human and automatic speech recognition, and analyzes an ASR front-end based on the extraction of localized, spectro-temporal patches from the speech signal with the aim of narrowing the gap between HSR and ASR (i.e., human and automatic speech recognition). In phoneme recognition experiments based on the Oldenburg Logatome Corpus, error rates of automatic recognizers were found to be more than 150 % higher than those of human listeners. This demonstrates the advances that have been achieved in the last decade of speech research (e.g., Lippmann (1997) reported an increase of errors by a factor of five for a similar task that does not utilize higher-lexical knowledge), but also shows the need for improved techniques to tackle the recognition problem.

5.1 Top-down vs. bottom-up processing

The overall gap between human and automatic recognition in terms of the signal-to-noise ratio was found to be 15 dB, i.e., the masking level for ASR has to be reduced by 15 dB to achieve the same performance as human listeners. By using resynthesized speech tokens in HSR (which were informationally equivalent to ASR features) this gap was divided in a bottom-up component of 10 dB (motivating the improvements of feature extraction presented in Chapter 4) and in a top-down component of 5 dB (cf. Fig. 5.1).

Recently, individual properties of top-down mechanisms have been incorporated into ASR systems (such as, e.g., algorithms for learning physiologically motivated features for optimal speech recognition, which relates to (long-term) learning of relevant speech cues (Chiu et al., 2009)). However, the majority of mechanisms playing a role in

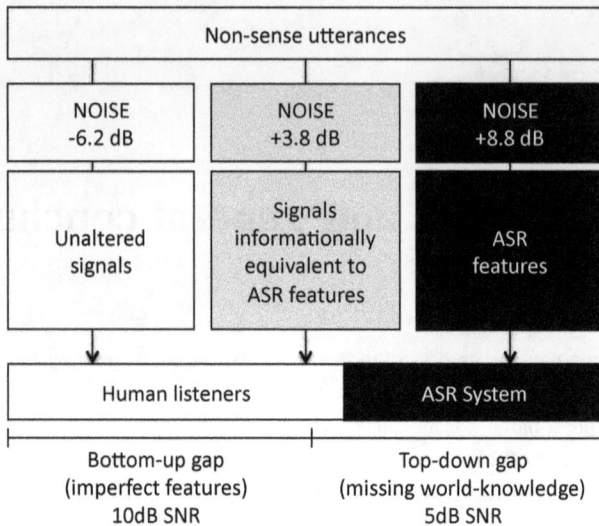

FIG. 5.1 *Separation of the man-machine-gap in the effects of bottom-up processing and the top-down component. For the depicted HSR conditions and ASR at this specific masking level, the same overall accuracy was obtained, i.e., the phoneme recognition rate was approximately 75 %. For this phoneme recognition task, the overall gap in terms of the signal-to-noise ratio was approx. 15 dB, for which feature extraction and classification contributed approx. 10 dB and 5 dB, respectively.*

top-down processing are not yet implemented in automatic recognizers. For example, human listeners use selective attentiveness to extract auditory cues cues that are likely associated with the desired acoustic target (Bregman, 1994). This is often based on specific knowledge about the target, which is not considered in the standard approach to ASR. The results presented in this thesis demonstrate that the classification bears room for improvement, which may serve as motivation to incorporate further aspects of top-down processing in ASR. Additionally, the quantitative comparison of the results obtained in HSR with resynthesized signals and ASR scores makes it possible to analyze specific weaknesses in common HMM-based classifiers.

5.2 Intrinsic variations of speech

The intrinsic variations that were parametrically changed in the Oldenburg Logatome Corpus (OLLO) were shown to affect both human and automatic recognition. In average, the influence of changes in speaking rate, effort and style had a similar effect on HSR as an increase of 1.5 dB of the masking level when a speech-shaped, stationary noise signal is used. In comparison, the disruptive influence on automatic recognizers was stronger: intrinsic variations resulted in the same overall degradation as an increase of the masking level by 5 dB. Furthermore, experiments presented in Chapter 4 showed that the average sensitivity of ASR towards intrinsic variations is comparable to the effect of a stationary masker at 0 dB (assuming matched training and test conditions). Confusions on the level of phonemes and articulatory features were however quite different for both types of variability, which indicates that different techniques will be required in ASR to cope with extrinsic and intrinsic sources of variation.

Large variations were observed between different studies that analyze phoneme confusions of men and/or machines. This shows that a direct comparison of absolute scores between experiments is often not feasible: Apart from factors such as the number and type of phonemes, the calculation scheme of the SNR (short-time SNR vs. long-term SNR), and differences between masking signals, the factor of across-speaker variability strongly contributes to the differences between studies, as talkers often employ different strategies when being asked to change their speaking style (Krause and Braida, 2003). In this context, the use of speech data recorded from the same speakers appears to be an important prerequisite in order to minimize unwanted variance of the recognition scores. The overall low robustness of ASR towards intrinsic factors was exemplary shown based on confusions of vowels with high and low speaking rate. While the errors in HSR were consistent over a wide range of signal-to-noise ratios, the ASR confusion patterns were less consistent even at relatively low masking levels. This inability of the ASR system to utilize duration cues in a similar way as employed in HSR suggests that temporal and spectro-temporal aspects of speech should be incorporated in ASR systems in a more appropriate way, which may for example be better suited to capture vowel transients.

5.3 Spectro-temporal features

The observations regarding insufficient processing of temporal cues in conventional ASR systems motivated the design and evaluation of a system based on spectro-temporal Gabor features. First, the robustness of optimized Gabor features (Meyer and Kollmeier, 2008) against a wide variety of (extrinsic) noise sources was demonstrated. The error rates compared to an MFCC baseline were more than halved when the recognizer was trained with clean speech, but tested with noisy utterances. Even when denoised MFCCs were chosen as baseline, Gabor features helped to increase the noise robustness in a stream combination experiment. An analysis of errors that occurred with MFCCs and spectro-temporal features showed that this was due to complementarity of these feature types. Experiments with the Oldenburg Logatome Corpus showed that this complementarity also extends to intrinsic variations: Spectro-temporal features performed well when the pitch was altered or the speaking effort was high. On the other hand, classic MFCC features yielded good performance when the speaking rate was changed. Finally, the analysis of confusions on phoneme level demonstrated that the feature types exhibit complementary properties regarding vowel and consonant recognition at high and low SNRs.

5.4 Future work

1. Improvement of ASR: One of the findings from the man-machine-comparison (Chapter 3) was the suboptimal recognition of specific articulatory features. This motivates further, well-defined changes to ASR features with the aim of improving robustness against intrinsic factors: For example, the degradations observed for increased and fast speaking style resulted from insufficient discrimination between voiced and unvoiced sounds. This shows that the sole use of the spectral envelope for the description of speech is not sufficient for an optimal recognition. Studies that investigated the fine structure of speech (i.e., the subtle and fine-grained, acoustic phonetic details of speech) strongly indicate that human listeners profit from such cues (Davis et al., 2002). The incorporation of such fine-phonetic features of the fine-structure is problematic in ASR, because it greatly increases the demand for training resources and computational cost. Therefore, a trade-off

between adding additional information of speech and the compactness of features is required. Due to their flexible properties and the wide range of parameters, Gabor features are possibly suitable to include some aspects of fine structure from the signal without overly increasing the feature dimensionality.

The use of spectro-temporal modulation filters presented in Chapter 4 was motivated by results both from the man-machine-comparison and physiological findings, which suggest that neuronal detectors for spectro-temporal modulations exist in the auditory system. From this line of research, two approaches that aim at an improvement of robustness of ASR follow directly: a) A combination of Gabor and MFCC features in ASR setups using multiple streams could exploit the observed complementarity and possible increase the performance in the presence of intrinsic variations. The comparatively simple combination of feature streams (i.e., the concatenation and subsequent decorrelation of feature vectors) could be replaced by state-of-the-art techniques used to select feature components based on non-linear neural networks, which merge the input of several input streams (as proposed in (Zhao and Morgan, 2008)) or feature selection algorithms such as sequential floating forward search (SFFS), which efficiently searches through very large parameter spaces (Pudil et al., 1994). b) Current approaches in feature selection (e.g., SFFS) could be employed not only for feature combination, but also to find suitable Gabor filter parameters. This could be combined with experiments that aim at increasing the overall robustness of Gabor features towards specific intrinsic variations (e.g., by incorporating speech material from the OLLO database for feature selection, in order to capture a larger number of modulation frequencies that allow for improved detection of transients in utterances with high and low speaking rates). In order to approximate the physiological ideal, a larger number than the currently used 80 filter prototypes could be employed, which has been shown to result in above-baseline results in other studies (Zhao et al., 2009).

An open question is why Gabor features alone are not suited to improve baseline results for some recognition architectures: Since the spectro-temporal filters can be tuned to capture purely spectral components (and thus potentially provide the same information that is supplied by cepstral features), an appropriate choice of filter parameters should result in scores similar to the baseline. Moreover, adding beneficial spectro-temporal and temporal feature components should result in a further increase of performance, thereby rendering cepstral features redundant. It might be due to the interaction of feature extraction and back-end which results in the fact that MFCCs are often required in stream experiments to improve the results: In the last 30 years a lot of work has been invested in the improvement of MFCC-HMM-classifiers, which is a highly optimized combination. When one of these components is replaced, it can therefore be difficult to achieve an improvement over this classic architecture, which resides in a 'local optimum' for a wide range of recognition problems. A second explanation might be the differences of recognition architectures, which are employed for the estimation of filter parameters (i.e., a linear neural net) and for the actual recognition task (i.e., a HMM or Tandem system). Due to the differences between these classifiers, the filter set obtained with the Feature Finding Neural Network might not be optimal for an HMM system, which could be solved by using the same classifier for optimization and recognition (at the price of higher computational requirements).

2. Modeling speech perception with ASR: Chapter 2 introduced a simple scheme for modeling phoneme confusions in HSR. In this approach, the difference of spectral properties of acoustic stimuli was employed to predict recognition and error rates. Despite the fact that other cues that are used by the human listeners were disregarded (e.g., the grouping of co-modulated signals across frequency channels (Festen, 1993), or the high temporal acuity of the auditory system that exceeds the temporal resolution of typically 10 ms in ASR (Turner et al., 1995)), this method was still suitable to explain for a large proportion of the variance of scores. This suggests following this approach by using the tools developed (i.e., the ASR framework combined with the Oldenburg Logatome Corpus) to build a model of human speech perception. Other studies that are in line with this research suggest that this might be a fruitful approach: Based on a model of human perception (Dau et al., 1996) and using a simple speech recognizer with a dynamic time warping algorithm, Jürgens and Brand (2009) showed that microscopic phoneme confusions can be well-modeled with a high precision, and that the speech reception threshold can be predicted with an accuracy of 1-2 dB. Barker and Cooke (2007) obtained good model predictions of microscopic

phoneme confusions based on methods traditionally used in ASR (i.e., hidden Markov models), combined with features mimicking the human ability to extract speech information from so called landmarks, i.e., regions above the noise floor that appear as patches in a time-frequency representation.

Although the focus of this thesis is not explicitly put on modeling human speech perception, the experiments presented in Chapters 2 and 3 establish the basis for the design of perception models: Stemming from data collected from normal-hearing subjects, an estimation of model parameters can be performed with the goal of predicting microscopic speech intelligibility. In this context, the use of the OLLO database offers several advantages: Due to the large number of speakers and utterances per speaker, it is well suited to perform the training of ASR classifiers that allow for a general representation of inter-speaker variability. Since the recognition task it to identify phonemes, the analysis of confusions can easily be performed based on articulatory features to gain insight into the nature of error patterns rather than analyzing the differences of specific classes of stimuli. Finally, the influence of intrinsic variations can be modeled, in order to analyze the basic properties of speech that exhibits increased speaking rate or effort or varying pitch. In future studies, the simple model based on spectral distance could be modified or replaced based on the approaches described above (i.e. models that better account for properties of the auditory preprocessing). The model could then be evaluated in the framework developed in this thesis, which consists of the recognition system that is trained and tested with the Oldenburg Logatome database in order to predict phoneme confusions and the influence of intrinsic variations in spoken language.

The speech database used in this thesis as well as the speech data collected in tests with human listeners have been made freely available for research purposes, with the hope of fostering studies that exploit the mutual flow of information between HSR and ASR, as schematically depicted in Fig. 1.2. The presented findings and provided tools may therefore serve to either improve automatic recognizers and to approach the goal of human-like recognition, or to build models of human speech perception, thereby contributing to our understanding of how our auditory system works.

Bibliography

Allen, J. (1994), "How do humans process and recognize speech?" IEEE Transactions on Speech and Audio Processing, 2, 567–577. 12

Barker, J. and Cooke, M. (2007), "Modelling speaker intelligibility in noise," Speech Communication, 49, 402–417. 38, 136

Benzeguiba, M., De Mori, R., Deroo, O., Dupont, S., Erbes, T., Jouvet, D., Fissore, L., Laface, P., Mertins, A., and Ris, C. (2007), "Automatic speech recognition and speech variability: A review," Speech Commun., 49, 763–786. 1, 53

Bregman, A. (1994), Auditory scene analysis: The perceptual organization of sound, The MIT Press. 6, 131

Chiu, Y. and Stern, R. (2008), "Analysis of physiologically-motivated signal processing for robust speech recognition," Proc. Interspeech, pp. 1000–1003. 5

Chiu, Y. B., Raj, B., and Stern, R. M. (2009), "Towards fusion of feature extraction and acoustic model training: a top down process for robust speech recognition," Proc. Interspeech, pp. 32–35. 5, 130

Cooke, M. (2005), "A glimpsing model of speech perception in noise," The Journal of the Acoustical Society of America, 119, 1562. 5

Cooke, M. and Scharenborg, O. (2008), "The Interspeech 2008 Consonant Challenge," in Proc. Interspeech, pp. 1781–1784. 1, 5, 12, 46, 53, 81, 87

Cooke, M. P., Green, P. D., Josifovski, L. B., and Vizinho, A. (2001), "Robust automatic speech recognition with missing and uncertain acoustic data," Speech Communication, 34, 267–285. 11

Dau, T., Püschel, D., and Kohlrausch, A. (1996), "A quantitative model of the "effective" signal processing in the auditory system: I. Model structure," The Journal of the Acoustical Society of America, 99, 3615–3622. 136

Davis, M., Marslen-Wilson, W., and Gaskell, M. (2002), "Leading up the lexical garden path: Segmentation and ambiguity in spoken word recognition," Journal of experimental psychology, human perception and performance, 28, 218–241. 87, 133

Bibliography

Davis, S. and Mermelstein, P. (1980), "Comparison of parametric representations for monosyllabic word recognition in continuously spoken sentences," IEEE Transactions on Acoustics, Speech, and Signal Processing, 28, 357–366. 54, 61, 102

De-Valois, R. and De-Valois, K. (1980), "Spatial Vison," Annual Review of Psychology, 31, 309–341. 95

Demuynck, K., Garcia, O., and Van Compernolle, D. (2004), "Synthesizing speech from speech recognition parameters," in Proc. Interspeech, pp. 945–948. 60, 63

Depireux, D., Simon, J., Klein, D., and Shamma, S. (2001), "Spectro-temporal response field characterization with dynamic ripples in ferret primary auditory cortex," Journal of Neurophysiology, 85, 1220–1234. 94, 122

Dimitriadis, D., Maragos, P., and Potamianos, A. (2005), "Robust AM-FM features for speech recognition," IEEE Signal Processing Letters, 12, 621–624. 125

Domont, X., Heckmann, M., Joublin, F., and Goerick, C. (2008), "Hierarchical spectro-temporal features for robust speech recognition," in Proc. Interspeech, pp. 4417–4420. 5

Dreschler, W. A., H, V., Ludvigson, C., and Westermann, S. (1999), "Artificial noise signals with speechlike spectral and temporal properties for hearing instrument assessment," The Journal of the Acoustical Society of America, 105, 1296. 106

Dreschler, W. A., H, V., Ludvigson, C., and Westermann, S. (2001), "ICRA Noises: Artificial noise signals with speech-like spectral and temporal properties for hearing instrument assessment," Audiology, 40, 148–157. 25, 63

Dubno, J. and Levitt, H. (1981), "Predicting consonant confusions from acoustic analysis," The Journal of the Acoustical Society of America, 69, 249–261. 16

Ellis, D. (2003), Rasta PLP in Matlab, URL, http://www. ee. columbia. edu/dpwe/resources/matlab/rastamat. 103

Ezzat, T., Bouvrie, J., and Poggio, T. (2007), "Spectro-temporal analysis of speech using 2-D Gabor filters," in Proc. Interspeech. 96

Festen, J. M. (1993), "Contributions of comodulation masking release and temporal resolution to the speech-reception threshold masked by an interfering voice," The Journal of the Acoustical Society of America, 94, 1295–1300. 136

Flege, J. E., Schirru, C., and MacKay, I. R. A. (2003), "Interaction between the native and second language phonetic subsystems," Speech Communication, 40, 467–491. 20

Fosler-Lussier, E. and Morgan, N. (1999), "Effects of speaking rate and word frequency on conversational pronunciations," Speech Communication, 29, 137–158. 11

French, N. and Steinberg, J. (1947), "Factors governing the intelligibility of speech sounds," The Journal of the Acoustical Society of America, 19, 90–119. 31

Garcia Lecumberri, M. L., Cooke, M., Cutugno, F., Giurgiu, M., Meyer, B., Scharenborg, O., van Dommelen, W., and Volin, A. (2008), "The non-native consonant challenge for European languages," in Proc. Interspeech. 90

Gelfand, S., Piper, N., and Silman, S. (1985), "Consonant recognition in quiet as a function of aging among normal hearing subjects," The Journal of the Acoustical Society of America, 78, 1198–1206. 16

Gramss, T. (1991), "Fast algorithms to find invariant features for a word recognizing neural net," in Proc. of IEEE 2nd International Conference on Artificial Neural Networks, pp. 180–184. 100

Gramss, T. and Strube (1990), "Recognition of isolated words based on psychoacoustics and neurobiology," Speech Communication, 9, 35–40. 100

Grant, K. W. and Walden, B. E. (1996), "Evaluating the articulation index for auditory-visual consonant recognition," The Journal of the Acoustical Society of America, 100, 2415–2424. 42

Griffin, D. and Lim, J. (1984), "Signal estimation from modified short-time Fourier transform," IEEE Trans. on ASSP, 32, 236–243. 62, 63

Handbook, I. (1999), "Handbook of the International Phonetic Association: a guide to the use of the International Phonetic Alphabet," . 108

Bibliography

Happel, M., Müller, S., Anemüller, J., and Ohl, F. (2008), "Predictability of STRFs in auditory cortex neurons depends on stimulus class," in Proc. Interspeech, p. 670. 95

Hazan, V. and Markham, D. (2004), "Acoustic-phonetic correlates of talker intelligibility for adults and children," The Journal of the Acoustical Society of America, 116, 3108–3118. 11, 42

Heckmann, M., Domont, X., Joublin, F., and Goerick, C. (2008), "A closer look on hierarchical spectro-temporal features (HIST)," in Proc. Interspeech, pp. 4417–4420. 96, 126

Hermansky, H. (1998), "Should recognizers have ears?" Speech Communication, 25, 3–24. 96

Hermansky, H. and Morgan, N. (1994), "RASTA processing of speech," IEEE Transactions on Speech and Audio Processing, 2, 578–589. 126

Hermansky, H. and Morgan, N. H. (1997), "Noise resistant auditory model for parameterization of speech," The Journal of the Acoustical Society of America, 101 (5), 2426. 11

Hermansky, H. and Sharma, S. (1999), "Temporal patterns (TRAPS) in ASR of noisy speech," in Proc. ICASSP, pp. 289–292. 89, 126

Hermansky, H., Ellis, D., and Sharma, S. (2000), "Tandem connectionist feature extraction for conventional HMM systems," in Proc. ICASSP, pp. 1635–1638. 101

Hillenbrand, J., Getty, L., Clark, M., and Wheeler, K. (1995), "Acoustic characteristics of American English vowels," Journal of the Acoustical Society of America, 97, 3099–3111. 88

Hirsch, H. and Pearce, D. (2000), "The AURORA experimental framework for the performance evaluations of speech recognition systems under noisy conditions," in Proc. ISCA ITRW ASR, pp. 2697–2702. 107

Hunt, M. (1999), "Spectral signal processing for ASR," Proc. ASRU 99. 6

Jacobsen, R., Fant, G., and Halle, M. (1952), "Preliminaries to speech analysis," . 108

Junqua, J.-C. (1993), "The Lombard reflex and its role on human listeners and automatic speech recognizers," The Journal of the Acoustical Society of America, 93, 510–524. 88

Jürgens, T. and Brand, T. (2009), "Microscopic prediction of speech recognition for listeners with normal hearing in noise using an auditory model," The Journal of the Acoustical Society of America, 125. 84, 136

Jürgens, T., Brand, T., and Kollmeier, B. (2007), "Modelling the human-machine gap in speech reception: microscopic speech intelligibility prediction for normal-hearing subjects with an auditory model," in Proc. Interspeech. 45

Kaernbach, C. (2000), "Early auditory feature coding," in Proc. of Contributions to psychological acoustics: Results of the 8th Oldenburg Symposium on Psychological Acoustics, pp. 295–307. 94

Kipp, A., Wesenick, M., and Schiel, F. (1996), "Automatic detection and segmentation of pronunciation variants in German speech corpora," in Proc. ICSLP, pp. 106–109. 21, 70

Kleinschmidt, M. (2002), "Methods for capturing spectro-temporal modulations in automatic speech recognition," Acustica united with acta acustica, 88, 416–422. 5, 8, 89, 96, 100

Kleinschmidt, M. (2003a), "Localized spectro-temporal features for automatic speech recognition," in Proc. Eurospeech. 87

Kleinschmidt, M. (2003b), "Robust speech recognition based on spectro-temporal processing," Ph.D. thesis. 96

Kleinschmidt, M. and Gelbart, D. (2002), "Improving word accuracy with Gabor feature extraction," in Proc. ICSLP. 5, 16, 38, 96, 100

Kliem, K. (1993), "Entwicklung und Evaluation eines Zweisilber-Reimtestverfahrens in deutscher Sprache zur Bestimmung der Sprachverständlichkeit in der klinischen Audiologie und Nachrichtentechnik," Ph.D. thesis. 16

Kohler, K. (1995), Einführung in die Phonetik des Deutschen (Introduction to German phonetics), Erich Schmidt Verlag. 18, 58

Kollmeier, B. (1990), "Messmethodik, Modellierung und Verbesserung der Verständlichkeit von Sprache ("Measurement, modeling and improvement of speech intelligibility")," Ph.D. thesis. 27

Kollmeier, B. and Wallenberg, E. (1989), "Sprachverständlichkeitsmessungen für die Audiologie mit einem Reimtest in deutscher Sprache: Erstellung und Evaluation von Testlisten (Speech intelligibility tests for audiology based on a German rhyme test: Development and evaluation of test lists)," Audiologische Akustik, 28, 50–65. 18, 59

Kollmeier, B., Kliem, K., and Wesselkamp, M. (1997), "Development and evaluation of a German sentence test for objective and subjective speech intelligibility assessment," The Journal of the Acoustical Society of America, 102, 2412–2421. 19, 59

Krause, J. C. and Braida, L. D. (1995), "The effects of speaking rate on the intelligibility of speech for various speaking modes (A)," The Journal of the Acoustical Society of America, 98, 2982. 53

Krause, J. C. and Braida, L. D. (2002), "Investigating alternative forms of clear speech: the effects of speaking rate and speaking mode on intelligibility," The Journal of the Acoustical Society of America, 112, 2165–2172. 44, 45

Krause, J. C. and Braida, L. D. (2003), "Acoustic properties of naturally produced clear speech at normal speaking rates," The Journal of the Acoustical Society of America, 115, 362–378. 11, 45, 56, 132

Leonard, R. (1984), "A database for speaker-independent digit recognition," in Proc. ICASSP, pp. 328–331. 54, 84, 104

Li, C.-n. (2003), "Accent, intelligibility, and comprehensibility in the perception of foreign-accented Lombard speech (A)," The Journal of the Acoustical Society of America, 114, 2364. 11

Lieb, M. and Fischer, A. (2002), "Progress with the philips continuous ASR system on the Aurora 2 noisy digits database," in Proc. ICSLP, pp. 449–452. 107, 119

Lippmann, R. (1997), "Speech recognition by machines and humans," Speech Communication, 22, 1–15. 1, 5, 12, 46, 52, 81, 93, 129

MacArthur, T. (1992), The Oxford companion to the English language, Oxford University Press. 17

Mesgarani, N., David, S., and Shamma, S. (2007), "Representation of phonemes in primary auditory cortex: how the brain analyzes speech," in Proc. Interspeech. 95

Meyer, B. and Kollmeier, B. (2008), "Optimization and evaluation of Gabor feature sets for ASR," in Proc. Interspeech. 8, 98, 132

Meyer, B., Wesker, T., Brand, T., Mertins, A., and Kollmeier, B. (2006), "A human-machine comparison in speech recognition based on a logatome corpus," in Workshop on speech-intrinsic variation, pp. 95–100. 24, 46, 63

Meyer, B., Wächter, M., Brand, T., and Kollmeier, B. (2007), "Phoneme confusions in human and automatic speech recognition," in Proc. Interspeech, pp. 1485–1488. 1, 12, 45, 93

Meyer, B., Wesker, T., Anemüller, T., Brand, T., and Kollmeier, B. (2009), "Human phoneme recognition as a function of speech-intrinsic variabilities," The Journal of the Acoustical Society of America, in review process. 59, 82, 86

Miller, G. and Nicely, P. (1955), "An analysis of perceptual confusions among some English consonants," The Journal of the Acoustical Society of America, 27, 338–352. 14, 28, 30, 42, 43, 48, 68, 108, 110

Mori, R. D., Deroo, O., Dupont, S., Jouvet, D., Fissore, L., Laface, P., Mertins, A., and Wellekens, C. (2007), "Intrinsic speech variations," Speech Communication, 49 (10-11), 764–860. 12

Mueller, C. (1992), "Perzeptive Analyse und Weiterentwicklung eines Reimtestverfahrens fuer die Sprachaudiometrie ("Perceptual analysis and development of a ryhme test for speech audiometry")," Ph.D. thesis. 16

Mühler, R., Ziese, M., and Rostalski, D. (2009), "Development of a speaker discrimination test for cochlear implant users based on the OLLO logatome corpus," ORL, 71, 14–20. 45

Peters, S., Stubley, P., and Valin, J. (1999), "On the limits of speech recognition in noise," in Proc. ICASSP, pp. 365–368. 54, 84, 85

Bibliography

Phatak, S. A. and Allen, J. B. (2007), "Consonant and vowel confusions in speech-weighted noise," The Journal of the Acoustical Society of America, 121, 2312–2326. 27, 34, 42, 48, 88

Pudil, P., Ferri, F., Novovicova, J., and Kittler, J. (1994), "Floating search methods for feature selection with nonmonotoniccriterion functions," vol. 2. 134

Qiu, A., Schreiner, C., and Escabi, M. (2003), "Gabor analysis of auditory midbrain receptive fields: spectro-temporal and binaural composition," Journal of Neurophysiology, 90, 456–476. 95, 122

Scharenborg, O. (2005), "Parallels Between HSR and ASR: How ASR can Contribute to HSR," Ninth European Conference on Speech Communication. 5

Scharenborg, O. (2007), "Reaching over the gap: A review of efforts to link human and automatic speech recognition research," Speech Communication, 49, 336–347. 5, 125

Schlueter, R. and Ney, H. (2001), "Using phase spectrum information for improved speech recognition performance," IEEE International Conference on Acoustics, Speech, and Signal Processing, 1, 133–136. 61, 85

Schukat-Talamazzini, E. G. (1995), "Automatische Spracherkennung," . 3, 4

Shen, W., Olive, J., and Jones, D. (2008), "Two protocols comparing human and machine phonetic recognition performance in conversational speech," Proc. Interspeech, pp. 1630–1633. 5, 52, 56

Shriberg, L. D., Kwiatkowski, J., and Hoffmann, K. (1984), "A procedure for phonetic transcription by consensus," Journal of Speech and Hearing Research, 27, 456–465. 46, 90

Siegler, M. and Stern, R. (1995), "On the effects of speech rate in large vocabulary speechrecognition systems," International Conference on Acoustics, Speech, and Signal Processing (ICASSP), 1, 612–615. 1, 12

Sroka, J. J. and Braida, L. D. (2005), "Human and machine consonant recognition." Speech Communication, 45, 401–423. 1, 5, 12, 42, 43, 46, 48, 52, 82, 86

Stern, R., Acero, A., Liu, F. H., and Ohshima, Y. (1996), "Signal processing for robust speech recognition," Automatic Speech and Speaker Recognition. Advanced Topics. 11, 53

Tchorz, J. and Kollmeier, B. (1999), "A model of auditory perception as front end for automatic speech recognition," The Journal of the Acoustical Society of America, 106, 2040. 11, 98

Ten Bosch, L. and Kirchhoff, K. (2007), "Bridging the gap between human and automatic speech recognition," Speech Commun., 49, 331–436. 12, 46

Turner, C. W., Souza, P. E., and Forget, L. N. (1995), "Use of temporal envelope cues in speech recognition by normal and hearing-impaired listeners," The Journal of the Acoustical Society of America, 97, 2568–2576. 136

Wang, M. and Bilger, R. (1973), "Consonant confusions in noise: A study of perceptual features," The Journal of the Acoustical Society of America, 54, 1248. 14

Weintraub, M., Taussig, K., Hunicke-Smith, K., and Snodgrass, A. (1996), "Effect of speaking style on LVCSR performance," Proc. ICSLP, pp. 1457–1460. 12

Wesker, T., Meyer, B., Wagener, K., Anemüller, J., Mertins, A., and Kollmeier, B. (2005), "Oldenburg Logatome Speech Corpus (OLLO) for Speech Recognition Experiments with Humans and Machines," in Proc. Interspeech, pp. 1273–1276. 45, 56, 105

Woodcock, K. (1997), "Ergonomics and automatic speech recognition applications for deaf and hard-of-hearing users," Technology and Disability, 7, 147–164. 2

Young, S., Odell, J., Ollason, D., Valtchev, V., and Woodland, P. (1995), "The HTK book," Cambridge University. 103, 107

Zhao, S. and Morgan, N. (2008), "Multi-stream spectro-temporal features for robust speech recognition," Proc. Interspeech, pp. 898–901. 96, 134

Zhao, S., Ravuri, S., and Morgan, N. (2009), "Multi-stream to many-stream: using spectro-temporal features for ASR," Proc. Interspeech, pp. 2951–2954. 135

Zhu, Q., Chen, B., Grezl, F., and Morgan, N. (2005), "Improved MLP structures for data-driven feature extraction for ASR," in Proc. Interspeech, pp. 2129–2132. 126

www.ingramcontent.com/pod-product-compliance
Lightning Source LLC
Chambersburg PA
CBHW021107210326
41598CB00016B/1363